Solving Church Education's Ten Toughest Problems

Solving Church Education's Ten Toughest Problems

John R. Cionca

VICTOR BOOKS®

A DIVISION OF SCRIPTURE PRESS PUBLICATIONS INC.
USA CANADA ENGLAND

All Scriptures are taken from the *Holy Bible, New International Version,*
© 1973, 1978, 1984, International Bible Society. Used by permission of
Zondervan Bible Publishers.

Library of Congress Cataloging-in-Publication Data

Cover Design: Bob Heimall Inc.

Cionca, John R., 1946–
    Solving church education's ten toughest problems/John R. Cionca.
      p.   cm.
    Includes bibliographical references
    ISBN 0-89693-787-9
    1. Christian education. I. Title. II. Title: Solving church education's ten
toughest problems.
    BV1471.2.C557 1990
    268—dc20   89-77942
                                                    CIP

2 3 4 5 6 7 8 9 10 Printing/Year 94 93 92 91 90

DEDICATION

In memory of Dr. Luke and Anna Sezonov,
my first pastor and his wife,
dedicated servants of Christ to His church.

CONTENTS

ACKNOWLEDGMENTS

I am grateful to the pastors' fellowships in Minnesota, New Jersey, and Arizona, who have interacted with me on their church education problems. In addition, appreciation must be expressed to the over 450 pastors who responded to my national survey on "C.E. Thorns."

I am thankful to Bethel Seminary for allowing me the privilege to research and write in relation to the courses that I teach. Similar recognition must be given to the Board of Church Ministries of the Baptist General Conference for their initial encouragement and publication of this writing project.

I am deeply appreciative to Mrs. Barbara McGaughey who word-processed my original manuscript, as well as the successive revisions.

And saving the best for last, I am most grateful to my wife Barbara, and to my children Ben and Betsy, who help me evaluate my priorities and teach me what life is all about.

PREFACE

Four years ago my interaction with pastors led me to write a chapter dealing with church problems in *What Every Pastor Wished He Knew About Music, Youth, and Education* (Word, 1986). Since that time I have surveyed other clergy associations, including a group of over 1,000 pastors, asking them to identify their most significant church education concerns. The results of these studies have been remarkably similar, and they serve as the basis for this book.

Solving Church Education's Ten Toughest Problems is not primarily a research report. The survey work was merely used to produce a rank order for the purpose of addressing the most common educational problems. I'm not so foolish as to believe that my analysis of these problems, or suggestions to help resolve them, are inerrant. However, I do believe the principles presented in each chapter address the heart of these issues, and offer hope for overcoming them.

Solving Church Education's Ten Toughest Problems is designed to show practical ways churches have successfully dealt with plaguing education problems. It is my hope that these principles will enable pastors, program leaders, and Christian education committees to analyze their own situations, and then adopt workable game plans for renewed educational ministries.

CHAPTER ONE

RECRUITING OF STAFF

Last week at Oakwood Fellowship[1] they combined classes in the junior high and high school for the third Sunday in a row. At Bethany Church the children attended the worship service with their parents, because there wasn't anyone to run the preschool church time. At Central Church three teenagers were pulled out of their Sunday School class to help in the nursery. If there is one predominant Christian education "thorn in the flesh," it's the recruitment of people to serve!

Several surveys of clergy, including a study of over 1,000 pastors, revealed the number one church problem is finding enough people to accomplish the educational program. But who's to blame for this crisis? Is it primarily spectator Christians who want to be ministered to, rather than to minister? Or has church leadership generated its own dilemma?

The merchant explains, "You get what you pay for." The farmer states, "You reap what you sow." I believe staffing is a problem in most churches because we have made it a problem. We are not victims of circumstance. Let me illustrate.

Many program leaders use impersonal means of recruiting workers, and then wonder why these people feel nobody cares. Frequently, churches seemingly abandon teachers to multiple years of service in one department. When these workers eventually quit, leaders wonder why the volunteers are not willing to take a new position. Pastors "cry wolf" from the pulpit so frequently that their appeals gain little response. Boards generate more programs than it is possible to staff. Churches buy into a cognitive model of education, which convinces people that they are not expert enough to teach. Publishing houses develop sophisticated materials for ordinary people, and wonder why these teachers struggle. It is true, we are reaping what we have sown: a numerically inadequate and insufficiently trained teaching staff.

One pastor assessed the problem this way: "When I do workshops on recruitment, I continue to be amazed at the haphazard way Christians are recruited for ministry. I am con vinced people are there to do the job, but need to be approached the right way." Another pastor admitted: "My greatest problem is dealing with people who could fill teaching positions, but are afraid to because they feel inadequate, or do not want to be 'stuck' in a position *ad infinitum.*

Do not despair, there is hope. Be assured of this fact: if poor practices have encouraged staffing problems, then the use of good procedures can also eliminate them.

Churches that have sufficient volunteers for their programs understand the dual nature of staffing: (1) the recruitment of new workers; and (2) the retention of effective teachers. A church that has a high retention in staff, will need very few new teachers. Conversely, the church that has high turnover, is continually seeking new personnel.

✱Any church that is finding difficulty staffing its C.E. program should ask several questions: (1) Does our church atmosphere encourage service? (2) Is our desired program staffable? (3) Do we have a vehicle for coordinating service? (4) Do program leaders know how to recruit prospective workers? (5) Are willing prospects adequately prepared for ministry? (6) Is prayer central to our staffing procedure?

The remainder of this chapter gives consideration to each part of this staffing checklist.

An Atmosphere That Encourages Service

When I worked in campus ministry, I would often hear students say, "I don't have to go to church to worship God; I can worship Him on a mountain." I agree with those students, but what they failed to recognize is that no one can grow in isolation. Spiritual maturity requires service to others. Jesus called servants into His kingdom, not lords. The greatest task of church leadership is not to fill a program vacancy; it's the broader task of opening people's horizons to the privilege of service. Developing the attitude that the "normal" Christian serves is fundamental to any recruitment efforts.

The picture of Christian service is painted by instruction and example. People must *hear* clear expositions of Scripture regarding the importance of service. I'm not talking about motivation by guilt, but rather the systematic explanation of personal stewardship aimed at heart and mind. Second, people will *see* service embodied before them. We can preach servanthood but until we provide opportunities for our people to observe it, we are only a sounding gong.

I am not implying that the church's leaders do not model service. But the average person in the pew does not perceive the totality of ministry, and therefore cannot imagine where she fits in. An atmosphere that encourages service helps people become aware of the substitute teacher, the woman who provides a casserole, or the teenager who keeps pencils, envelopes, and visitor cards, neat and well-stocked. Effective recruitment begins with opening people's eyes to the diversity of service and possible roles for themselves.

The pastor can use the *pulpit* to emphasize the importance of ministering to one another. Some pastors offer prayers of commitment for C.E. workers, or share positive feedback received from parents. Others illustrate sermons with examples gleaned from teachers.

The *church newsletter* can cultivate a positive attitude toward service. A periodic lead article from the pastor lets members know that he personally values the educational ministry of the church and esteems those who serve in it (an example of this type of article follows the end of this chapter). Each newsletter can also highlight a particular ministry. The article should inform people about the program, but can also commend those workers who are serving faithfully in that department. A "Focus on Youth" for example, may relate current themes of study, but will also seek to boost the image of the staff team.

The *family of God* is another means of exposing service. In my former church the adult choir would recess for the summer. In their place a different person each week would speak. My concern was threefold: (1) to introduce another member of our growing church family; (2) to have him share a brief testimony clear enough so that a non-believer in the congregation could understand how to become a Christian; and (3) to illustrate that all the parishioners served someplace. The family of God helped people realize that "average people like me" can minister in the church.

A *membership seminar* can do more than introduce people to the uniqueness of a local fellowship; it should also encourage ministry. For example, the last session of our membership class presented "Service in the Body of Christ." After a biblical presentation on personal stewardship, I would frankly state: "We are not involved in a Sunday School contest, or trying to impress anyone with statistical growth. You are free to participate in church services without being a member. However, if you desire membership, then we expect you to be an active member, and that means serving in this local assembly. For the sake of this fellowship, but also for your own spiritual growth, I encourage your participation."

Our application for membership requested personal information on one side, and service information on the reverse. People were encouraged to check several ministries that were of interest to them. Assurance was given against overcommitment, yet assistance was provided for finding a meaningful role. Those desiring to follow through with membership would meet with two elders to share their statement of faith and discuss their serving Christ form. (An outline for a session on church service, and a sample talent survey, are located at the end of the chapter).

Exposure to *teacher training* is another way to paint vision. While teacher training is typically designed to improve the skills of people already involved in a program, I frequently encourage others to attend these sessions. Exposing prospective volunteers to fellow Christians who are serving helps them catch a vision. As a result, some will take their first step toward personal ministry. When people know they can attend a class, no strings attached, they are more likely to accept our invitations to observe a session, view a video, or attend a seminar.

There are many other ways to build an atmosphere conducive to service. One church schedules a *kick-off dinner* after a morning service in the early fall. The dinner is open to everyone, and they use video recordings and live presentations to overview the whole educational ministry. In another assembly the pastor makes it his practice to highlight a ministry each month during the *announcement time*. Several congregations conduct a church-wide *ministry fair* to make people aware of their educational programs. A few churches highlight their programs on slides, while one larger church builds booths to display each ministry. Another pastor mentioned that his fellowship uses their *home Bible studies* to disciple young Christians, and to encourage them to become aware of areas where volunteers are needed.

There are many ways to expose people to the value of service. But motivation through guilt is not as productive long-term as cultivating a positive environment where service is viewed as normal and beneficial for personal growth.

A Staffable Program

After my wife and I were married we towed a 4' x 6' U-Haul to Denver. Two years later we left seminary for Arizona in a small Ryder truck. Eight years later we moved to New Jersey. This time our belongings were loaded into half of a United Van Lines trailer truck. Six years later we moved to Minnesota filling nearly all of a 45' Allied van. Interestingly enough, my last move will be in a 2' x 6' box. How is it that we collect so much baggage in our journey through life? While that's a subject for another book, let me suggest how the same phenomenon occurs in churches.

Christians in the early church met in homes; three centuries later they owned common property and buildings. Over the years the buildings escalated in size, as did programs and budgets. The Sunday evening service is a primary example. With the invention of the coal-gas light (1792), American churches added Sunday evening services. Since these new lamps were too expensive for private use, curiosity seekers flocked to public buildings that illumined the night. Pastors began evangelistic services that were targeted to the many nonbelievers who would not attend a morning service. Today, most churches are experiencing a serious decline in their evening service attendance, and very few view the programs as evangelistic. Yet this once vibrant, relevant form is now part of our institutional baggage.

In addition to the traditional A.M. and P.M. services, most churches have added a Sunday School. Next, youth meetings were developed, followed by children's church time. Vacation Bible Schools have become a staple, and club programs are proliferating.

Music ministries beyond the adult choir have also flourished. It is common in a number of large churches to have several choirs, handbell groups, orchestras, and ensembles.

Ushering has developed from a pick-up game just before the offering, to an orchestrated team effort, seating people, and distributing bulletins (wherever bulletins came from). And don't forget the adult dinner committee, the silver anniversary committee, the library committee, as well as the dozen or more standing committees required by constitutions.

Fifty years ago we didn't solicit people to lead the cherub choir; 100 years ago we didn't burn out teachers in the club programs; and 1,800 years ago we didn't need personnel for the decorations committee.

I'm not saying we should strip out all our programs. In fact, I advocate specialized ministries for church growth. But the question still remains: "When is enough, enough?" Some churches may have a larger program, while others of necessity must have a smaller program. The key is how much program a congregation can realistically staff. No church can do everything well.

16

Choirs, committees, and clubs all compete for the same human resources to keep them going. Beyond this, most churches do not even acknowledge that some of their members should minister outside of their local flock, as ambassadors to the larger church and to the lost. Realistically speaking, each congregation must decide for itself if its program is staffable. And equally important, it must make sure it is using volunteers for only the most essential ministries.

A Vehicle for Coordinating Service

How long has Alice Smith taught the juniors? Would Bob Reed like to do something other than ushering? Has Janet Clark ever been asked to serve? Unless a church has a system for tracking service, and a strategy for coordinating recruitment efforts, it will never realize its staffing potential.

If we are *convinced* that a Christian cannot be all that God wants him to be unless he's ministering to others, then we must be certain that everyone is given opportunities to serve. A simple record card or computer entry for each member can track service by detailing an individual's ministries over the years, both within and outside of the church.

A record system for registering service should not be restricted to the education department. Unfortunately, many new congregants are bombarded by indiscriminate requests from the youth coordinator, choir director, nursery chairperson, and club leaders, while others are overlooked altogether. Our right hand must know what our left hand is doing.

A good record system is best maintained by one person responsible for that ministry. The person should sit on a personnel committee consisting of ministry heads and the senior pastor. In the smaller church these program leaders are volunteers, whereas in a larger church they are frequently members of the professional staff. In either situation the coordination process is the same. In one Midwestern church the program directors meet weekly to discuss individuals for possible areas of ministry.

Developing a service record system will not take place overnight. As new members enter the church, a new entry should be recorded (including service in former churches). Longer-term members can be surveyed through their Sunday School classes, or even during the morning worship service. For example, one church did this with a bulletin insert, filled out during an extended offertory. This kind of information is best received, however, through honest personal involvement with members. The average congregation has staffing difficulties because it has not taken the time to develop a balanced program, and because it does not truly know the backgrounds, aspirations, fears, involvements, and potentials of its people. Through these one-on-one visits leaders can communicate that they are primarily concerned with congregant's growth.

Now you're possibly thinking, "Wait a minute, Bill Barclay would blow up if he knew we kept a record of his service, or more accurately stated, his lack of service!" I agree, but the person who voices greatest resistance to this system is likely the person who needs it the most. Perhaps Bill had been contacted five times, and five times he refused to serve. Typically these people are allowed to remain as "deadwood." But they, too, are saints that must be equipped. The notations on Bill's record card or computer entry would serve as a reminder for concerted prayer on his behalf by the leadership.

Classes need teachers, children need caretakers, widows' homes need to be painted and the church ministry needs prayer support. There is not a single person in the congregation who cannot make a ministry contribution. Just as the disciples went from door to door teaching the Gospel, so too we need to take the message of service into the homes of our members, especially the inactive ones. If this endeavor leads a person to withdraw from membership, then the church will be better off in the long run. Christ reminded believers that He would rather they be hot or cold, but not lukewarm. With this conviction we must draw people into service, and a record system helps in the process.

A Proper Approach with Contacts

All too frequently churches solicit people for service through general SOS appeals from the pulpit, or through the bulletin.

In the hallway, in a classroom, or even in the sanctuary, people have been pressured into teaching. One pastor accurately observed that "general pleas for volunteers cheapens the ministry and gives little motivation for service (usually guilt is the driving force). Individuals should have the joy of being offered a ministry that they carry out with a genuine sense of call."

Placing the right people in the right jobs eases the long-term burden of recruitment, because it reduces teacher turnover. Another pastor expressed it this way: "Even though recruitment is our major problem, it is also our strongest point. We choose our leaders carefully, looking for Spirit-filled, vision-oriented people. Their dedication solves a lot of problems."

I believe there are some *prerequisites for recruitment.* First, it is essential to have *job descriptions,* or at least position analyses. How can people prayerfully consider a ministry when the particulars of that ministry have not been explained. The prospective teacher has a right to know the details of a job, its length of tenure, and available resources. While there are many different forms for these descriptions, I prefer a simple four-part format.

The job description begins with a "definition" of the position. Second, "relationships" are defined. (Who is the supervisor of the worker? What is his/her relationship to the board? How long is the term of appointment?) The largest section of the description delineates the "responsibilities" of the position. Perhaps as many as seven to twelve very specific statements of behavior are spelled out precisely. Last, "qualifications" needed for the position are noted. If the person must be a member, the description should state such. If certain skills are needed (e.g., tactfulness, ability to lead people, or a deep love for children), these should be expressed. A sample job description is included at the end of chapter 8.

A second prerequisite for recruitment is the *service contract.* I believe there is value to making one-year appointments to service. This procedure enables those responsible for staffing to know the tenure of their commitment. Near the completion of each contractual period, workers can agree to another year of service, change areas of ministry, or take a short break between ministry terms. Since people's schedules change frequently, this procedure shows understanding and respects the commitments of our people. A sample appointment to service form is included at the end of this chapter.

In addition to prerequisites for recruitment, let me describe some *principles of recruitment.* First is the *principle of exposure.* The more visible the recruiter, the more likely he or she will receive a favorable response from the contact. A person is more likely to say yes to a friend or someone with whom she is familiar, than to a stranger. Where trust and integrity are already established, the volunteer is more likely to believe that the recruiter is not just interested in filling a vacancy. Exposure may be through the recruiters reading of Scripture from the pulpit, or the participation in Sunday School class socials. Success in recruitment is related to the prospective worker's familiarity with the recruiter.

The *principle of sowing* is another way to express the importance of recruiter visibility. The more we sow by way of relationships with people, the more we will reap from them. While this sounds selfish and manipulative, this is not the case. Remember, our primary motivation is to help people grow through meaningful service. Filling a ministry opening is a means to assist them. A program leader who is friendly in the hallways of the church, makes home visits, invites people for dinner, or sends a card or note, will more likely succeed in recruitment.

The *principle of team spirit* also facilitates recruitment. A program leader only concerned with his own staffing needs does not help the overall program, as much as a leader who is sensitive to several ministries. Some recruiters try to pressure people into an area of service regardless of the prospect's desire or giftedness. This practice rarely produces a long-term worker. Much better is this approach: "I understand, Bob, you would rather work with teens than children. Let's pray that God will lead you into a meaningful area of service, and let me also mention to Bill Swanson, our youth coordinator, that you might be interested in doing something with our youth."

Invitations in recruitment begin with *setting up an appoint-*

ment. Churches that report success in recruitment indicate that they approach workers on a one-to-one basis. "Hello, Bill, this is Fred Johnson, the director of our Battalion program. We've been having a great time with our boys, and because of our growth we want another man to join our leadership team. Our pastoral staff thought you might enjoy this type of ministry, and suggested I make an appointment to describe the club. Our meeting would not put you under any obligation to make an immediate commitment. In fact, we would want you to have a week to talk and pray about it with Barbara. I need about thirty minutes of your time to explain our program. Would you have either 8:00 or 9:00 available next Wednesday evening?"

At the meeting, Fred began on a motivational note, stressing the importance of the club in leading boys to Christ and discipling them. Then he described the format of the program. Next he worked through the job description, which specifically explained what he wanted Jim to do. He noted that the appointment to service was for one year and then clarified the resources available to assure Jim's success (Fred's own availability, their monthly leaders meeting, and the fall training program). The leader concluded his time with Jim in prayer, indicating that he would call him in a week to learn of his decision.

Fred's *follow-up contact* was by telephone, and he subsequently shared Jim's response with the personnel committee. Since Jim was willing to undertake this new ministry, Fred began helping him prepare for the classroom.

Early Preparation for Service

Our Lord Jesus ministered among many people. Vast crowds witnessed His miracles and heard His teachings, and some of them responded to His invitation, "Follow me." In Mark's Gospel we observe Christ's strategy for training: "He appointed twelve—designating them apostles—that they might be with Him and that He might send them out to preach" (Mark 3:14). Jesus used a modeling and field education approach to teaching. Long before the Great Commission, and even before

21

His men were sent out two by two, the disciples had been *with* Jesus, observing Him.

What a contrast is practiced in many churches. Frequently volunteers barely say yes, when a mysterious book, called a quarterly, is shoved into their hands, and they are thrust into the lion's den.

New Christian education workers benefit greatly from observing class sessions prior to assuming responsibility for their own class. In fact, many program leaders encourage the observation of one or two teaching sessions before they ask a potential volunteer for a commitment. Whether they observe a live teaching situation, or view a class on video, new teachers will profit from seeing and discussing examples of what is expected of them. A comprehensive approach to teacher training is given in Chapter 3. Recruiters must understand the positive connection between early preparation and successful recruitment. A church that is serious about recruitment will ease people into their new teaching responsibilities.

Ongoing Intercessory Prayer

Prayer is last in our consideration, not because it is less significant, but because it is so critical to recruitment. The prayer life of Jesus serves as an example for all believers, especially for those who lead His church.

The Gospel accounts record that *Jesus prayed about the twelve.* Before He selected His disciples he spent all evening in prayer (see Luke 6:12ff). It is naive for a program leader to approach a prospective worker without first bathing that encounter in prayer.

Second, *Jesus prayed in the presence of the twelve.* Before breaking bread, Christ prayed; after ministering to the crowds, he prayed; at the raising of Lazarus, he prayed. So noticeable was his prayer that the disciples asked Him, "Teach us to pray" (Luke 11:1). Teachers should pray with their students; program leaders should pray with their workers; and personnel committees should pray by name for prospects. Jesus not only prayed about the twelve, but He demonstrated prayer in their presence.

Third, *Jesus prayed continually for the twelve.* In his high priestly prayer Christ prayed specifically for his disciples (John 17). Even with the crucifixion weighing heavily upon Him, Jesus still interceded for another (see Luke 22:32). Similarly, committed program leaders will not just pray about prospective volunteers, but will continue to intercede for specific, ongoing needs of their staff.

Fourth, *Jesus asked the twelve to pray.* Our Lord's challenge to the disciples is equally applicable to us: "Watch and pray so that you will not fall into temptation" (Matt. 26:41). There is no greater temptation to those involved in recruitment than to first speak to people about the ministry, rather than to first speak to God about these people. Do we really believe we can succeed in staffing while neglecting His command: "Ask the Lord of the harvest, therefore, to send out workers into His harvest field" (Matt. 9:38)?

Because prayer is so central to staffing, we dare not restrict intercession to the personnel committee or program leaders. One pastor, for example, periodically prints requests and distributes them to "the pastor's prayer corps," a group of people specifically committed to intercession. Just as Jesus asked the Twelve to pray, we too must make prayer the center of our staffing efforts.

Conclusion

Last year Woodcrest Church members again had staffing problems, but this year for the first time they have every C.E. position filled! They recognize they're not out of the staffing woods for good. In fact, four months from now they face twelve possible vacancies, not counting the special education class they want to start.

But their people are cultivating healthy attitudes toward lay ministry. From the pastor to the class secretary, they have fostered an atmosphere that gives prestige to service. Their existing staff believes they are doing an eternal work, and prospective workers are exposed to these ministers regularly. As a church they are positively praying for others to answer the call to service.

Will Woodcrest Church fulfill their staffing needs for next year's program? I'm confident they will. Your church can do the same.

---

[1]The examples given in each chapter are drawn from specific congregations, though sometimes they are composites drawn from several congregations. While the names have been changed, they represent actual church situations.

A Checklist for Recruitment

Does our church have . . .

☐ An Atmosphere That Encourages Service

☐ A Staffable Program

☐ A Vehicle for Coordinating Service

☐ A Proper Approach with Contacts

☐ Early Preparation for Service

☐ Ongoing Intercessory Prayer

Sample Newsletter Lead Article

"PASTORAL EPISTLE"

"Your Serve?!"

Recently I saw my fourth-grade Sunday School teacher. He is one of those special men who has shaped my life. Believe it or not, he has prayed for me every day since I first entered his class 33 years ago!

Would you be available to shape a child's life? We still have over 100 openings for teachers and helpers to minister in our children's ministries this fall. The greatest need is during the 9:45 A.M. Sunday School hour, but other opportunites are at 8:30 and 11 A.M. and 6 P.M. on Sundays, plus Wednesday evenings.

The reasons to say "no" are many: "I'm busy." "We don't want to miss our adult congregation." "Sure don't want to be tied down each week!" "Too new to Wooddale." "Already served my time—let someone else do it!"

The reason to say "yes" is one: We are disciples of Jesus who "came not to be served but to serve."

Don't wait to be asked. Volunteer! (Call Children's Director Catharine Coon or write a note on your registration card.) When asked, say "yes."

For the children's sake.

For your sake.

For Jesus' sake.

It's your serve!

—Pastor Leith Anderson

The article is from The Wooddale Witness, *of Wooddale Church, Eden Prairie, Minnesota. Its value is three-fold: It communicates a need for teachers; it affirms that the pastor values church service; and it gives visibility to the Children's Minister (the one who will make recruiting contacts). Used by permission.*

Sample Article Promoting
Educational Programs

Highlighting the Twos and Threes Dept.

One of our newest SS departments is our early childhood twos and threes. Prior to last June two-year-olds were included in our toddler nursery, and at that time parents were very happy to learn that their two-year-old children would now be offered a total morning Bible-centered program. Trinity's two- and three-year olds are studying "I Learn of Jesus," a course which is specifically designed for their learning capabilities and interests. Learning centers, Bible stories, Bible activities, music, refreshments, handwork, and choosing activities are all a part of the morning schedule.

Barbara Cionca is the Superintendent of the twos and threes department, and her 9:45 teachers are: Bob Anderson, Mae Bailey, Blanche Frye, and David Poppy. The 11:00 teaching staff consists of: Barbara, Carol Himes, Moris Ambri & Linda Schult.

If you are interested in observing the teaching world of our two's and three's, you are more than welcome to contact Barbara Cionca for a time when you may observe.

These articles from The Trinity Caller, *Mesa, Arizona inform the congregation as a whole that good things are happening in the educational ministry. Second, they keep parents up-to-date on those who are working with their children, and what they are learning. Third, they function as a low-key, positive reminder that service is rendered by ordinary, everyday Christians who love the Lord and love his church. Used by permission.*

Outline on Church Service

"STEWARDSHIP IN THE CHURCH"

I. OUR POSITION IN CHRIST
(2 Cor. 5:17): Because He has blessed us with all spiritual blessings, our hearts respond with the desire to serve.

II. THE LORD'S OWNERSHIP
(Ps. 24:1-2; Rom. 14:3): Since He owns everything, my time, talents and resources are actually His.

III. THE CHURCH'S MINISTERS
(1 Cor. 1:1-2; 2 Cor. 3:5; 2 Cor. 5:18): Christ has given the ministry of reconciliation to all believers, therefore every member is a minister of the church.

IV. THE BODY OF CHRIST
(1 Cor. 12:12-27): All Christians are members of the Body of Christ, and for the Body to function, all must become actively involved.

V. THE PRINCIPLE OF FAITHFULNESS
(Matt. 25:14-30): Believers are accountable and will be judged for how they manage the time, talents and resources that God has entrusted to them.

VI. THE EXAMPLE OF STEWARDSHIP
(Mark 10:45; John 13:35): If Jesus did not come to be ministered unto, but to minister, we also should serve.

VII. STEWARDSHIP OF FINANCES
(Luke 16:10-13; Matt. 6:19ff): Use the worksheets on "the Christian and finances" to establish your personal plan for giving.

Sample Talent Survey

SHARED MINISTRY SURVEY

Home:

_____

Street Address   Apt. #   Home Phone #

_____

City   Zip

ADULT CONGREGATION in which you are involved:

☐ College/Career (TJ)   ☐ Ambassadors (UE)   ☐ Voyagers (UC)
☐ Navigators (UD)   ☐ Mariners (UB)   ☐ None (UN)
☐ Pilgrims (UA)   ☐ Crusaders (UF)

I am presently involved or want to serve in the following ministries:

WORSHIP SERVICE ASSISTANCE	Presently Involved	Want to Serve	MUSIC	Presently Involved	Want to Serve
Usher	NA ____	PA ____	Choir	NE ____	PE ____
Greeter	NB ____	PB ____	Other Vocal Music	NF ____	PF ____
Sound System/Video	NC ____	PC ____	Instrumental Music	NG ____	PG ____
Drama	ND ____	PD ____	Drama	NM ____	PM ____

CONGREGATION MINISTRIES			YOUTH MINISTRIES	Presently Involved	Want to Serve
Congregational Leader	NH ____	PH ____	Jr. High SS Teacher	EN ____	FN ____
			Sr. High SS Teacher	EP ____	FP ____
Adult SS Teacher	NJ ____	PJ ____	Son City Volunteer Staff	EQ ____	FQ ____
Discovery Class Leader	NK ____	PK ____	Jr. High Volunteer Staff	ER ____	FR ____
Visitor Follow-up	NL ____	PL ____	Jr. High Junction (7th & 8th gr.)	ES ____	FS ____
			Sr. High Son City (9th - 12th gr.)	ET ____	FT ____
MISSIONS COMMISSION			Son City Transportation	EU ____	FU ____
Commission Member	LG ____	MG ____	Bus Driver (retreats & special events)	EV ____	FV ____
Promotion	LH ____	MH ____			
Communication w/ Missionaries	LJ ____	MJ ____			
Administrative Volunteer	LR ____	MR ____			

Sample Talent Survey Continued

CHILDREN'S MINISTRIES	Presently Involved	Want to Serve	SMALL GROUP MINISTRIES	Presently Involved	Want to Serve
Children's SS Teacher	EA _____	FA _____	Growth Group Leader	GA _____	HA _____
Children's Asst. SS Teacher	EW _____	FW _____	Growth Group Member	GB _____	HB _____
SS Teacher Substitute	EB _____	FB _____	Men's Discipleship Leader	GC _____	HC _____
SS Teacher Summer Substitute	EC _____	FC _____	Men's Discipleship Group Member	GD _____	HD _____
Special Education Teacher/Helper	ED _____	FD _____	Women's Discipleship Leader	GE _____	HE _____
Nursery Worker	EE _____	FE _____	Women's Discipleship Group Member	GF _____	HF _____
Nursery Worker Substitute	EF _____	FF _____	Homemakers' Group Leader	GG _____	HG _____
Nursery Committee	EG _____	FG _____			
Children's Church Teacher	EH _____	FH _____	Homemaker's Group Member	GH _____	HH _____
Children's Church Aide (4th grade & older)	EK _____	FX _____	Homemaker's Children's Program	GJ _____	HJ _____
Pioneer Girls Volunteer Staff	EJ _____	FJ _____	Homemaker's Nursery Worker	GK _____	HK _____
Pioneer Girls Pal	EK _____	FK _____	Women's Ministries "Circles"	GL _____	HL _____
Pioneer Boys Volunteer Staff	EL _____	FL _____			
Vacation Bible School Teacher	EM _____	FM _____	**TECHNICAL**		

TAPE MINISTRY					
			Carpenter/Cabinet maker	AE _____	DE _____
			Electrician	AF _____	DF _____
Duplicating	LA _____	MA _____	Painter	AG _____	DG _____
Recording	LB _____	MB _____	Plumber	AH _____	DH _____
Cataloging	LC _____	MC _____	Heating/Cooling	AJ _____	DJ _____
Tape Desk Clerk	LC _____	MD _____	Grounds	AK _____	DK _____
			Graphic Arts	AL _____	DL _____
SOUND	AP _____	DP _____	Printing	AM _____	DM _____
			Photography	AN _____	DN _____

AUDIOVISUAL	AQ _____	DQ _____
LIBRARY	LE _____	ME _____

PASTORAL CARE AND COMMUNITY SERVICES

CHURCH NEWSLETTER					
			Visitation to elderly, home-bound, handicapped	LK _____	MK _____
Typing	AR _____	DR _____	Transportation to medical & business appointments for seniors, etc.	LL _____	ML _____
Mailing	AS _____	DS _____			
Writing/Editing	AT _____	DT _____			
Layout	AU _____	DU _____			
Word Processing	AV _____	DV _____			

30

CHILDREN'S MINISTRIES	Presently Involved	Want to Serve	SMALL GROUP MINISTRIES	Presently Involved	Want to Serve
ADMINISTRATION			Emergency Services	LM ___	MM ___
		DA ___	food, clothing,		
Computer/data entry	AA ___	DB ___	shelter, advocacy		
Typist	AB ___	DC ___	& help at holidays		
Receptionist	AC ___	DD ___	Clothing Shelf	LN ___	MN ___
Personnel	AD ___		help staff		
Recruitment		DO ___	Food Shelf	LP ___	MP ___
Mailing	AO ___		help staff		
			PRAYER CHAIN	LQ ___	MQ ___

Adapted and used by permission of Wayzata Evangelical Free Church, Minneapolis, Minnesota. The letter coding has been set up for computer processing.

Appointment to Service Form

MY COMMITMENT TO SERVE
IN CHRIST'S CHURCH

As a Christian education worker, I will:

- Follow the leading of the Holy Spirit in my daily life.
- Maintain the spiritual disciplines of prayer and study of the Bible.
- Participate in congregational worship and fellowship.
- Cultivate caring relationships with nonbelievers.
- Serve faithfully according to the responsibilities in my position description.

I understand that my commitment is for the period of September 1, 1990 to August 31, 1991.

Please sign two copies, then return one copy to your program leader, and keep one copy for your own record of commitment.

Name _____ Date _____

CHAPTER TWO

POOR FOLLOW-UP OF PUPILS BY TEACHER

What is a teacher? Someone may respond, "a person who teaches a lesson" Another may insist, "someone who helps students learn." Do you see any difference between those definitions? The first definition focuses on the teacher, while the second focuses on the pupil. The first can describe the person who lectures from a Sunday School quarterly, but the second necessitates an individual who helps the student understand and apply a biblical concept.

The two answers illustrate a fundamental difference of viewpoint about the role of a teacher, and point to the major reason pastors identify "poor follow-up of pupils" as their second greatest education concern.

One pastor expressed it like this: "Without a doubt, for me the greatest challenge is encouraging teachers and club leaders to have contact with their kids during the week between church exposures. I don't think I have one club leader or teacher who has caught the vision and importance of getting into the homes of children and adults to better understand all the facets of the students' lives." Another pastor expressed his frustration this way: "Our teachers don't visit, don't have socials, and are not interested in contacting visitors or absentees."

Dr. Henrietta Mears has said, "The teacher has not taught until the student has learned." I agree with her. While some teachers follow a practice based on the first definition, the nature of our Christian message demands that we follow the higher definition of teaching. Our focus must always be on the student and the growth of his or her relationship to Christ. This type of teaching requires more than instruction, it necessitates knowing the students we instruct.

Jesus illustrated this principle when he stated that the Good Shepherd knows His sheep, and that they know Him (John 10:14). Similarly, the teacher who wants to guide students must know them, and they in turn must know him. Yet this type of relationship is the exception rather than the norm in most church programs.

Guiding students into Christlikeness is enhanced by a long-term relationship between teacher and learner. A teacher who drops his responsibility at the end of a class period cripples learning. Yet, for many churches the problem goes even deeper. Some congregations get so far behind in the recruitment and retention of staff that they adopt a quarterly, monthly, or weekly teacher rotation. This practice is not in the best welfare of the student. In this schedule teachers will rarely accept "ownership" of their class. They do their thing for God, drop their content, and then leave.

How can a church break out of this rut? How can a congregation encourage teachers to be more than in-class instructors? How can it help them assume responsibility for caring beyond the classroom?

The pastor looking for a quick fix for staffing problems, will not find a good solution. If he tries some quick fix, it may help him in the short term, but will likely burn his people for the long run. The same is true regarding a teacher follow-up program. Several good principles worked on over time will produce a lasting result not possible by a quick fix.

Let me share six principles that will encourage our teachers with follow-up. A teacher-shepherding ministry can be a reality for the church that develops: a shared-ministry concept; an accountability system; examples of shepherding; a specific ministry assignment; resources for shepherds; and celebration of success.

A Shared-Ministry Concept

Whose responsibility is it to teach and care for the members of the church? Most people would answer, "the pastor." While I agree with that response, let me also stress the need for the whole congregation to share in service. Teachers will more likely accept responsibility for student follow-up if their church as a whole believes that ministry belongs to the entire congregation.

When Paul wrote to the Corinthians, he actually addressed all Christians "everywhere who call on the name of our Lord Jesus Christ" (1 Cor. 1:2). Under the guidance of the Holy Spirit, he stated that each believer was given a gift of the Spirit for the common good (1 Cor. 12:7). Therefore the active service of every Christian is just as important to the congregation, as a body part is necessary to the whole body. In his second letter he reminded the church that Christ "died for all, that those who live should no longer live for themselves but for Him who died for them and was raised again" (2 Cor. 5:15). Living for Christ cannot be separated from living for others: "Whatever you did for one of the least of these brothers of mine, you did for me" (Matt. 25:40). A shared-ministry concept was encouraged by Paul when he wrote: "Therefore, if anyone is in Christ, he is a new creation; the old is gone, the new has come! All this is from God, who reconciled us to himself through Christ and *gave us the ministry* of reconciliation" (2 Cor. 5:17-18, emphasis mine).

All Christians have been given the ministry of reconciliation. The pastor is not the only minister in the congregation; all are ministers. All are directed to bear with one another (Eph. 4:2), encourage one another (1 Thes. 5:11), instruct one another (Rom. 15:14), and be devoted to one another (Rom. 12:10). A church that desires effectiveness in shepherding, must realize that it is more than just the pastor's responsibility. Time will not permit the pastor to teach and care for everybody. Nor will his spiritual gifts allow him to handle all aspects of ministry equally well. Even personality factors will hinder him from developing relationships in the same way with all people.

35

Why is it that a shared-ministry concept is not fully practiced in most churches? In some situations the problem lies with the pastor. He wants to make the first hospital call, lead the services, decide directions, and be the hub around which the ministry centers. But even if a pastor can preach, do special music, collect the offering, lead hymns, teach a combined Sunday School class and do all the visitation, he would still be ineffective. There are in every congregation people who can do some of those functions better. And even if they cannot do them better, failure to equip people for service will, in the long run, hinder their spiritual growth.

In other situations the problem lies with the laity. Some congregations believe only the pastor can minister. In fact, some make their view perfectly clear when they resound, "That's what we pay you for!"

A look at the New Testament reveals that even Jesus did not practice a solo ministry. He sent out the seventy two by two and commissioned the disciples to go and make disciples. This multiplication process has continued through the pages of church history to the present. The congregation that continually teaches and models a shared-ministry concept will find more of their teachers adopting the responsibility of caring for students.

An Accountability System

Most churches have a procedure for the follow-up of visitors or absent members. The problem many face, however, is that their procedure is not *comprehensive* enough to care for everyone all of the time. As one pastor expressed it: "Too often people fall through the cracks. It's not unusual for us to find someone was hospitalized, or someone has left the church, well after the event had taken place."

A *good format* used by many churches for follow-up is the dividing of their membership among church board members. But this format provides little or no oversight for visitors or nonmembers, who frequently comprise nearly one-third of the congregation.

A *better format* for follow-up is to take advantage of the

already established Sunday School structure. Teachers of children can give oversight to their students, and the well-functioning adult department offers even greater potential for consistent follow-up. Churches that use an elective format have greater difficulty tracking people than churches that use a stage-graded adult format. In the stratified approach, all adults, whether they attend Sunday School or not, can be placed in subcongregations. Each class leader is responsible for the care of everyone within that age fellowship. Since teachers in the children and youth grades also follow up their students, many families in the congregation will have contact from two sources.

The *best format* for follow-up is a combination approach that utilizes both adult Sunday School classes and the church board. For example, when Southwood Church moved from electives to a stage-graded class structure, an elder was assigned to each of the five new classes. Each smaller congregation eventually had a teacher, class leader, and an elder representative. Regular attenders, new visitors, the less involved, and those with special needs were all channeled to their respective class leaders for follow-up.

A comprehensive system is a must for follow-up, but *accountability* within the system is equally critical. Contacts with visitors and other special calls are channeled by the class leader to several people interested in caring. If awareness of the need begins at the class level, they handle it directly; if it comes from another member or through the pastor, the class also follows up. Accountability takes place as the class leader reports to the pastor or at the monthly board meeting. For example when Alice Clark went to the hospital to have her baby, the class leader of the Homebuilders lined up members of the class to provide meals for Alice's first week home.

Regular meetings help assure accountability. Throughout the month class leaders and deacons should make the pastor aware of situations that require his personal attention. Furthermore, the agenda of the monthly board meeting includes a review of what is happening in each of the small congregations.

Teachers working with children have a similar vehicle for

37

accountability in their monthly staff meetings. While each teacher is responsible for his or her own Sunday School class, the monthly meeting is the place where the department leader follows up on how the teachers are following up. The atmosphere at these meetings is not heavy; the purpose is not to heap guilt on those who are negligent. Rather they are times of information, rejoicing, and ongoing prayer for individual students.

The weekly use of *records and report forms* helps teachers and program leaders stay abreast of developments in the classroom. Accountability forms should not encumber teachers, but simply assist them in tracking student absenteeism.

Good records begin with a comprehensive class roster. This is not an enrollment record which may include someone who hasn't attended the church in years. Rather, it's a realistic listing of people who should be cared for by the class. Since a copy of absentees is also made for the program leader, weekly follow-up on the teacher's follow-up is possible (sample attendance records are included at the end of this chapter, but several types of systems are available through your local Christian bookstore).

Attendance patterns should be reviewed at department meetings in the children's division, or likewise at the adult leaders' meeting or board meeting. Expressions of concern noted on the form provide items for prayer. In addition, team leaders can plan a strategy for ministering more effectively to their students.

Examples of Shepherding

If we want our teachers to shepherd their students, then pastors and program leaders must do a good job of shepherding their teachers. Unfortunately, willing personnel are often quickly recruited and then stuck in some remote classroom—never again remembered until, in burnout, they ask to resign. Follow-up and caring *by* teachers will rarely happen, until follow-up and caring *of* teachers is first taking place.

After a teacher's first class session, a wise program leader will check to see how the class time progressed. Upon coming across a good article, the thoughtful leader will make a copy for a teacher who would profit from it. A personal note or card for a special occasion goes a long way in building camaraderie.

Thoughtfulness is also expressed by the leader who asks a teacher if some time off is needed. If there is a sickness within the worker's family, the caring program leader will call or visit, or perhaps prepare a meal for the family. When the pastor and program leaders demonstrate caring, teachers see shepherding ways they can imitate.

A Specific Ministry Assignment

Terry Freezen is a single woman who serves in her church's club program, works in children's church and sings in the choir. Fred Guthrie serves on the board of elders at his church, teaches an adult Sunday School class, chairs the stewardship committee, sings in the choir, and leads a home Bible study. I admire the commitment level of Terry and Fred; I am amazed at their ongoing service and cheerful spirit. However, I am also concerned for them.

Terry and Fred typify the deeply committed in our churches who are sacrificially giving much of their time in many arenas of service. When people give that much time to church programs, I begin to wonder if their own needs and other responsibilities are being met. How often do they feel ministered to, or are they always the ones being spent?

The average blue-collar worker gives forty-nine hours per week on the job; the average white-collar employee invests sixty-two hours per week. Gone is the pipe dream of the four-day work week. For most people, time is their scarcest commodity. Do members have enough time for their family or friends? Are they cultivating relationships with unbelievers? And even regarding their church service, are they able to do the best possible job in each area of responsibility?

A congregation that wants to develop a shepherding ministry through its teachers must make realistic ministry assignments. It must also guard against the proliferation of church activities that compete for the worker's participation. While we may want our best leaders to serve as church officers, I believe we often tie up these gifted people in administrative detail. A church that desires intentionality in its shepherding ministry must reduce the workload of its people so that their primary responsibility is their teaching and follow-up. Some congregations can accomplish this by reducing the amount of meetings in a calendar year. Many churches, however, will need to streamline their governing structures so that fewer people run the routine operation, freeing them up to spend more time with people.

When a church tries to reduce worker load, it often finds that it has several jobs for which it has no personnel. While this is frustrating initially, let me suggest that it is a long-term blessing. First, the new situation will force some to look for additional people to fill those ministry openings (not the already overworked). Second, it may lead the church to realize that they are offering more programs than they can realistically staff.

Are your leaders expected to attend services on Sunday morning, Sunday evening and Wednesday night; attend committee meetings, teacher training sessions, home discipleship groups, and even other programs? If so, it's possible that the overall church programming is interfering with the worker's ability to do his best in teaching and shepherding.

In addition to commitments at the church, people have obligations related to their jobs, school, neighborhood, family, and friends. With all of those responsibilities, follow-up of students can get overlooked.

Many people are involved in community activities outside of the local church, and this is good for believers. But if reducing a teacher's responsibility at the church simply means that they add additional responsibility from a parachurch or local organization, we may have defeated our own purpose. Church leaders need to help teachers plan for balance in their responsibilities. If a person's primary ministry is in a neighborhood shelter, then they must have enough freedom to do that job well. Likewise if a congregant's ministry is teaching a Sunday School class, they also need enough time for follow-up of those they teach.

Resources for Shepherds

A church has every right to ask its teachers to follow up students, but it also has an obligation to help teachers with that responsibility by providing resources to assist them. The greatest resource the teacher needs is *time,* and we've just suggested how teachers and leaders need realistic schedules. This is so critical that a wise church will periodically schedule seminars on time management, personal goals, and the art of self-discipline.

A second resource helpful to teachers is *training in follow-up.* Just as some people feel inadequate about personal evangelism, some teachers feel uncomfortable making home visits. They wonder what they should say to pupils, or their parents, especially if a parent is unchurched. Program leaders can model home visitation by accompanying hesitant teachers. The monthly department meeting is a great place for discussions on outreach. Since the sharing of successful visits is highly motivational, these staff meetings are a good place to help newer teachers catch a vision for follow-up.

In addition to time and training, many churches assist teachers by providing *materials* for shepherding. Some Sunday Schools supply their teachers with cards to send notes to absent students; others even provide postage stamps. A number of churches purchase bulk subscriptions to Christian magazines for their teachers. One pastor indicated that he selects and gives a good commentary to the adult teachers to supplement their quarterlies. Over time the teachers begin to develop good reference libraries. Another church periodically mails a relevant booklet to their teachers, just to let them know they are thinking of them.

There are many materials available to help volunteers with their teaching and follow-up. A church makes a good investment of its money when it budgets for resources for teachers.

Before we move from the topic of resources, let me make a bold suggestion. While it's appropriate for a church to provide follow-up materials for its teachers, let me suggest that we encourage teachers to develop their own *personal ministry funds.* This account becomes part of their annual family bud-

41

get, and is above the amount given to the church. The amount may be small at first, but when they discipline themselves to work up to 1 or 2 percent of their annual income, they will have ample funds for carrying on their personal ministries.

With this fund they may purchase a commentary for class preparation. They may use part of the money to buy a gift for a sick child. They may tap the fund to take their class out for a social activity, or provide a dessert fellowship in their home. The ministries account may also be used for babysitting expenses when they go on visitation.

A ministries fund is beneficial to both the teacher and church for several reasons. First, if this type of money is not budgeted (either by the church or the teacher), quality shepherding will not likely take place. The youth sponsor just cannot afford the $37.50 to have the junior high kids over for pizza.

Second, teachers will not feel "taken advantage of," if the money they use for ministry is already budgeted. When a worker keeps shelling out for postage, shower gifts, or other materials with money she does not have in her own budget, resentment may produce a negative feeling about her service.

Third, when the volunteer uses his own ministry account, he becomes more involved and excited about what's taking place in students' lives. Remember, Jesus taught that where our treasure is, that's where our heart is. As we invest our money into specific people, our heart is drawn to an even deeper commitment to them.

Any efforts that are made to assist teachers with their shepherding will let them know that they are appreciated.

Celebration of Successes

Research studies demonstrate how people live up to our expectations. For example, the teacher who believes he has a group of exceptional students will typically grade them higher than the teacher who believes he has a group of less capable students. In the story of *The Little Engine That Could,* the little switcher repeated, "I think I can, I think I can, I think I can." As a result he actually did pull the cars up the mountain! Similarly, in the area of outreach and caring, people who have said, "I think I can, I think I can, I think I can," actually do reach out!

Obviously, a deeply introverted person will not become a charismatic leader. We all have certain parameters and comfort zones related to our personalities and experiences. Nevertheless, teachers who think they can make some strides in the area of follow-up or shepherding will see their dreams realized.

Teachers can be helped to *think they can* by celebrating the successes of those who are reaching out. For example, on my way to church one Sunday I noticed one of our members helping a woman and her children with their disabled vehicle. I was proud of Larry, and later mentioned to the congregation how his example typified who we are—servants of Christ. Our people realized that caring *is* taking place daily, and they need to believe, "Yes, I can do it too!"

In daily ministry to people we will encounter heartbreaks and happiness. While we remember in prayer the apathetic student, or the adult who does not want involvement or intimacy, we cannot afford to let those negative experiences drain our enthusiasm. Regular outreach leads to profitable home visits, supportive hospital calls, and other types of meaningful encounters. The wise program leader highlights these successes, and helps his staff catch a vision for shepherding.

Conclusion

You have heard the expression: "The rich get richer, and the poor get poorer." It appears that the same holds true in ministry. Ministry-rich congregations become more effective, while ministry-poor churches become more impoverished. Success breeds success. A church that begins to care beyond the classroom will begin to view itself as a caring church. In turn, as they think of themselves as a caring congregation, they will demonstrate even more caring.

A church that is struggling with the follow-up of students by teachers must move away from bemoaning its situation and target a positive game plan for shepherding. As successes are celebrated and further encouraged, regular shepherding by teachers (and all of the congregation) will continue to grow.

A Checklist for Effective Follow-Up

Does our church have . . .

☐ A Shared-Ministry Concept

☐ An Accountability System

☐ Examples of Shepherding

☐ A Specific Ministry Assignment

☐ Resources for Shepherds

☐ Celebration of Successes

Sample Record Forms

SUNDAY SCHOOL REGISTRATION CARD
(High School & Down)

NAME _____ DATE _____

ADDRESS (Street) _____

CITY & STATE _____ PHONE _____

PARENTS' NAMES _____

CHURCH MEMBER ___ YES ___ NO

CHURCH NAME _____

HOME CHURCH ADDRESS _____

AGE _____ DATE OF BIRTH _____

GRADE IN SCHOOL _____

ASSIGNED TO: DEPARTMENT _____

_____ EARLY SS _____ LATE SS

REMARKS _____

TBC-102   REGISTRAR _____

This form is used to register children and teen visitors *to the Sunday School. The triplicate NCR paper allows copies for the teacher, program leader (lead teacher), and the office. Used by permission of Trinity Church, Mesa, Arizona.*

45

Sample Record Forms
(Continued)

CLASS REPORT

DATE _____ CLASS _____

TOTAL PRESENT _____

NO. OF TEACHERS _____ NO. OF MEMBERS _____

NO. OF VISITORS _____

ABSENTEES   VISITORS

_____ _____ _____ _____

_____ _____ _____ _____

_____ _____ _____ _____

_____ _____ _____ _____

_____ _____ FOLLOW-UP for Absentees & Visitors

_____ _____ 1st week—Make a phone call. (Ph)

_____ _____ 2nd week—Make a mail contact. (MI)

_____ _____ 3rd week—Home or personal. (PC)

Distribution: Office Copy—White   Lead Teacher—Canary   Responsible Teacher—Pink
TBC-103

This form is used for follow-up of visitors and absent class members. *The triplicate form NCR paper assures accountability by providing copies for the leader, program leader (lead teacher), and the office. Used by permission of Trinity Church, Mesa, Arizona.*

CHAPTER THREE

TEACHER TRAINING

Wouldn't it be great to have every staff position in your church filled? In fact, since we're dreaming, let's add a willing substitute to each department. But wait a minute, while staffing is important, staffing with competent workers is more important. In fact, poor teachers may hurt a church more than shortage of staff. *Any warm body won't do!*

Any warm body won't do, because *students need to learn God's Word.* In the Scriptures there is life, and children, teens, and adults must be ignited with this biblical truth. A poor Sunday School teacher will hinder learning by boring students with the Bible. Rather than seeing a living message, they are turned off by irrelevant lessons that are poorly communicated.

Any warm body won't do, because *the church has purposes to accomplish.* Members of the body of Christ participate in "worship," care for one another in "fellowship," reach out to the lost in "evangelism," and teach the Scriptures through "education." These purposes are the reason the church exists, and their accomplishment requires volunteers actively serving. In every area of the church, Christians must be equipped to minister, and that includes teachers.

Any warm body won't do, because *teachers need fulfillment in their ministry.* Workers who lack confidence or feel incompetent do not experience joy in their service. If they feel ineffective with their students, unable to motivate them with the Scriptures, they become discouraged. But teachers who know their subject matter, use appropriate methodologies, and have good rapport with students find their classroom experience a highlight of each week. Training leads to competence, confidence, and joy in service.

Training helps *new teachers* understand effective means of instruction. It shows them how to orchestrate the classroom environment and how to handle classroom control. Training offers practical insights on what works, and doesn't work, to make learning come alive for students.

Training also helps *veteran teachers* stay fresh in their approach. Creatures of habit fall into ruts; they gravitate to that which is comfortable. Systematic training exposes even tenured teachers to new formats or methods that can add freshness to their classrooms. This new enthusiasm for teaching, in turn, heightens student interest in the class.

Many churches try teacher training, but get frustrated with their attempts. As one pastor noted: "We have difficulty getting adult Sunday School teachers to realize their need for continued training. While many have a good grasp of the Bible, they are ineffective in communication skills." Another pastor lamented: "Our board feels that teacher training is paramount, but our training sessions are not well attended because teachers do not see training as important." Yet another minister expressed it this way: "Teacher training and motivation continues to be a difficult part of my job. Too many have the attitude that a nominal effort will produce good results. However, a nominal effort produces nominal results and a poor education program for the church."

While experiences such as these are prevalent among churches, they are not universal. Though some congregations are struggling with their training programs, other churches are having success in teacher development. There will always be some resistance to trying new things (training), and people's schedules will always be full; nevertheless, a church with a comprehensive game plan for training will help its teachers improve in their ministry skills. A comprehensive approach to teacher training includes meaningful content; high expectations; a variety of formats; a spirit of camaraderie; sufficient finances; and a coordinator of training.

Meaningful Content

Time is a precious commodity. Since people value their time, they will not waste it on trivial meetings. If a teacher is required to attend a training session, then the program had better be worthwhile. Each meaningful training experience lends credibility to the training program. Each meeting that does not have a meaningful content will erode participation. Because of human nature and our fast-paced life, the erosion process moves more quickly than the building process. Programs that minister personally to teachers, and help them better minister to others, will stimulate regular participation.

Training for teachers should address a number of concerns. Topics worth reviewing include:

- The teacher's spiritual life
- Developing teaching confidence and competence
- Becoming a better student of the Bible
- Understanding our learners
- Maximizing student involvement
- Appropriate teaching methods
- Moving from explanation to application
- Classroom control
- Extending teaching session beyond the classroom
- New resources for communication
- Measuring teaching effectiveness

When each training session is a winner, teachers are more likely to return for further training. They are also more likely to enthusiastically promote the program to any who missed the training. Meaningful content fosters teacher receptivity for ongoing training.

A Variety of Formats

There are many means available to a church for developing its teaching staff. The training format used by a congregation will vary according to the needs of its teachers. If workers show that they need help in lesson planning, then monthly department meetings can assist them. If a number of teachers are having difficulty with a common problem (e.g., classroom discipline), then a larger group session is appropriate. If the staff needs motivation, then a local seminar or guest speaker would be beneficial. A variety of formats exist for accomplishing teacher training.

The *department meeting* is the backbone of any teacher improvement program. A typical department meeting brings together three to six members who work in a specific program. For example, the group may be the women who work with third- and fourth-grade adventure clubs, or the couples who work in the twos-and-threes Sunday School. These small groups usually meet once a month to evaluate past programs, review student needs, plan next month's program and study specific teaching techniques.

● *Planning* is the predominant feature of a monthly meeting. Based on their understanding of learner needs and lesson objectives, teachers can decide "who will do what" for the upcoming class sessions. For example, workers in the fours-and-fives department can decide who will tell the story, who will work at each learning center, and whether Bible activities will be in large or small groups. Those working in the club program might decide who will handle the recreation, who will lead the group time, and who will hand out the awards. A well-run program is one that is well-prepared.

● *Training* occurs (almost subliminally) as teachers plan together by following the suggestions in their teaching manuals. Specific training can also be structured into the monthly session. Workers can view a video of a model lesson; they can discuss a good magazine article; or they can study an ingredient of the learning process.

● *Prayer* is also an important feature of the department meeting. Members of some teaching teams take time to each share a ministry concern and a personal concern. Then each worker prays for the person on his or her right. Over a year (or several years) the teaching team grows close to one another. Their ministry is more than an assignment; it becomes a spiritual boost and warm fellowship.

Annual in-house training provides opportunity for the church's entire teaching team to expand their learning skills. For example, Biscayne Church conducts training for its entire staff on four Thursday nights in July. Calvary Church plans five training sessions throughout the year, calling it the "5-50 Protection Plan" (see brochure at the end of this chapter). A number of churches schedule an all-day workshop on a Saturday. A typical schedule might look like this:

  8:30 Registration, Beverage, Rolls
  9:00 General Session
10:30 Session One
11:45 Lunch
12:30 Session Two
  1:45 Break
  2:00 General Wrap-Up (or Session Three)

A format like the one above combines both inspiration and instruction. A resource person could lead all four sessions, or one or more of the sessions could be used for stage-graded or topical electives. A quality in-house training experience will benefit from the following suggestions:

• Plan well in advance (12 months).

• Get the most qualified and stimulating speaker possible, from as close a distance as possible (reduced travel expenses can be added toward a worthy honorarium).

• Announce at department meetings that participation is required, but also contact each teacher individually.

• Prepare name badges ahead of time, with extra badges available for those who may show up unannounced.

• Monitor room arrangements and equipment needs (adequate seating, room temperature, projectors, handouts).

• Make certain that refreshments and lunch are of good quality, and are served on time.

• Following the seminar, send notes of appreciation to the staff for giving valuable time to sharpen their teaching skills.

One-on-one training opportunities are profitable for assisting individual teachers with specific needs. Frequently it is the personal touch that makes one business thrive over another. Similarly, personal interaction with teachers not only gives special guidance, but it also strengthens the relationship between leader and worker. Together they may view a video teaching session, stopping periodically to discuss what is taking place. Or they might meet over coffee to consider a student's needs, or a classroom situation that keeps occurring.

Program leaders who spend time each week reading good periodicals and books are in a position to pass on some of their gleanings. For example, a teacher may offer: "Let me give you this booklet on building esteem in children. After you read it, let's get together and talk about it." A short book or timely article is usually well received by teachers. The one-on-one approach makes the worker feel: "My leader really does care about me and my teaching responsibility."

While large-group training helps many people with relatively little of a program leader's time, one-on-one training uses a maximum amount of the leader's time, but in the long run produces a well-trained, well-cared-for teaching team.

Observations and evaluations unfortunately are seldom used. Nevertheless they are insightful means of training. Teachers will benefit from *observation* of other classroom settings (i.e., decorations, layout, resources, table arrangements, etc.); and specifics of instruction (how the story is told, activity pages, learning centers, guided conversation, etc.).

Observations of competent teachers in one's own church are profitable, but the pastor or program leader can also make arrangements for workers to observe other church settings (an ongoing reciprocal practice can be established among several churches). Teachers can grow in their own skills by observing what is happening in other learning environments.

Evaluations, though rarely practiced, can also develop teaching competence. Assessments of classroom demeanor provide an objective view of teaching strengths and weaknesses. Listening to a cassette recording of one's own teaching is the least threatening type of observation. Teachers can then consider their instructions (were they clear?), their methods (were they appropriate?), their students (were they involved?), or their communication (were lesson objectives reached?).

Several churches have followed a program whereby annual evaluations are part of their training format. In these congregations teachers are recruited knowing they are expected to participate in both observations and evaluations. While many teachers are anxious about outside observers, most will find the evaluation process helpful once they have tried it. (For a fuller discussion of teacher evaluation, including forms for assessing the teaching-learning process, see pp. 171–189 of my *Trouble Shooting Guide to Christian Education*. Denver: Accent Books, 1986.)

Sunday School conventions have been a part of the Christian education scene for several decades. While the quality of conventions varies from region to region (and sometimes from year to year), they have remained a good source for teacher training. The typical area-wide convention serves two purposes: (1) It is highly motivational; and (2) it is practically instructional.

Christian education *conventions are motivational* in a couple of ways. First, the general sessions are usually led by noted Christian educators, chosen because their enthusiasm for teaching is contagious. Second, the participation of many churches together helps workers see that they are part of a larger picture. The gathering of hundreds of teachers for training is in itself highly motivational.

Sunday School *conventions are also instructional.* Scores of "how to" sessions give teachers practical ideas applicable to their own class situations. Courses such as "Understanding Preschoolers," "Music in the Sunday School," "Discipling Teens," "Building the Adult Department," and even "Making the Library Effective" are typical convention workshops.

Christian education congresses are relatively inexpensive. Program coordinators and workshop leaders usually donate their time. Publishers that send consultants to advertise their latest products also make them available to teach a few workshops. A typical registration fee might be $5 compared to $40 for a professional seminar.

A drawback of these conventions is the conflicting concepts sometimes presented by the volunteer leaders. The following experience illustrates this lack of a unified philosophy of education. A preschool teacher attended one workshop where the instructor emphatically stated that good teachers should be able to keep children's attention focused on a story for thirty minutes. At the next session a different leader discussed the importance of using a variety of methods, "because young children do not have long attention spans." While this type of inconsistency is infrequent, it is a possibility with a diversity of leadership.

In general, the local Christian education convention is a beneficial means of providing training for a church's Christian education workers. The financial cost to the church is minimal, and the planning time investment of the pastor or program leader is almost nil. With convention dates publicized well in advance, teachers (and even prospective workers) can make themselves available for this training opportunity.

Regional seminars are additional off-campus opportunities profitable for teacher development. For example, the Walk Thru the Bible seminars help teachers with an understanding of the Old and New Testaments. Seminars from Scripture Press Ministries provide practical age-level training. Churches Alive, Campus Crusade for Christ, the Navigators, Youth Specialties, and other organizations all conduct regional seminars helpful to a teaching staff.

Many Christian colleges and seminaries offer *continuing education classes* (as well as regular credit courses) that are open to non-degree students. Teachers find participation in these class settings very stimulating. The quality of instruction and the caliber of students make these credit courses thoroughly enjoyable.

High Expectations

An interesting phenomenon takes place in many congregations. New people attending a church may at first go to all the services. But after several weeks they begin to disappear on Sunday evenings. It's as if the new folk look around at the smaller crowd and come to the conclusion, "I guess we're not supposed to be here after all."

A similar experience can occur in some teacher training programs. The meetings may have meaningful content, but when teachers are permitted to be absent, the whole staff is negatively affected. It is important, therefore, that those responsible for training (program leaders, superintendents, or even the pastor—depending on the size of the church) expect 100-percent participation of teachers at the meetings. If a training meeting is worth having, then it's worth requiring the presence of every worker.

The first place to instill the expectation of total participation is in the recruitment process. The job description should explicitly state that teachers are expected to participate in all department training sessions and other annual training events. The purpose for these meetings should be explained to the prospective teacher, and reviewed with continuing teachers when they re-sign their annual commitments. Teachers who have been negligent in training (without valid excuses for their absence) should not be reappointed for another term of service. Remember, any warm body won't do in the cause of teaching God's Word to God's people.

While high expectations increase teacher involvement, unrealistic expectations dampen it. For example, Brookdale Church scheduled a major training emphasis each fall, but it also required attendance at weekly department meetings. Each Wednesday evening the staff met together to plan the following Sunday's lesson. Though some churches experience success with this format, Brookdale felt it had a negative long-term effect on teachers. Their climbing student-teacher ratio (25:1) illustrated their staffing difficulties. Two service meetings a week (Sunday School and Wednesday evening) kept some teachers from personally being fed. This neglect, in turn, led to burnout and hindered retention.

A more realistic approach to training might include one or two whole staff meetings per year, and department meetings monthly. Some churches adopt a training calendar which lists all training dates for the entire year (see example at the end of this chapter). Early scheduling of all-staff training is a must, for it will encourage the maximum number of people to attend these important events. Monthly planning meetings can be scheduled whenever it is convenient for the program staff. It's a rare group of three to six people who cannot coincide their schedules for a one- to two-hour meeting per month.

Since credibility is built by consistency, only in extreme circumstances should a training event be canceled. High expectations for participation at both faculty training and department training foster regular teacher participation.

Spirit of Camaraderie

The teachers at Los Altos Community Church demonstrate a deep commitment to training. While their good participation over the years is related to the high quality of training provided by the leadership, there is another subtle ingredient at work at Los Altos—the teachers like each other.

A worker will usually attend a training session that appears meaningful. She is even more likely to participate if her friends are also going. A department that has a genuine camaraderie among its teachers finds its workers willing to meet on a regular basis, while the department that is experiencing tension among its staff will find its workers resistant to, (or absent from), group meetings.

A healthy team spirit begins with the program leader who displays the attitude: "You people are the greatest—I really enjoy being with you." Then as teachers develop into a caring team, the monthly department meeting moves beyond mere lesson planning. Decorating bulletin boards changes from a chore to a creative activity; discussions on students switch from negative complaining to positive strategies and intercessory prayer. A spirit of camaraderie is a subtle, yet essential, component of any training emphasis.

Sufficient Finances

We are all familiar with the expression, "What's the bottom line?" Most meaningful ministries incur a program cost, and this is true for an effective teacher training program. Sufficient finances are necessary for books, filmstrips, videos, speakers, registration fees, and recognition banquets.

Several times I have been asked to identify the most important contribution I made to the church education program at Trinity Church. Jokingly, yet with an element of seriousness, my response has been: "I doubled the Christian education budget within the first three years." In actuality, the most important contribution was the building of positive team attitudes; yet even those attitudes could not have been cultivated without adequate resources. The cards, pamphlets, and even books sent to teachers as expressions of appreciation, were made possible because of the healthy Christian education budget. Seminar fees were underwritten, and appreciation banquets were first-class, all because of sufficient funds for teacher development.

I am amazed that many churches establish a conference/training account for their pastor, yet budget little or no money for training the laity. The pastor has already attended three or four years of seminary, but the lay person has had little or no theological training. The pastor only preaches thirty minutes each Sunday, while teachers have up to sixty minutes for instruction. Who has the greatest need for conferences and training? A church that takes seriously its educational task must also accept the responsibility to budget liberally for effective training.

A Coordinator of Training

Which of the teachers in your church have led people to Christ? Who are the ones with a good understanding of the Old Testament, or the New Testament? How many have participated in a Sunday School convention, or attended a training seminar? Which teachers do a good job with classroom control? While a program leader might be able to answer these questions about his own department, it is a rare congregation that knows all of its people this well. Yet effective training takes advantage of the expertise of one another, and this necessitates coordination.

Too often people view training as something leaders do with teachers. But leaders are not the only ones who can give helpful assistance. Some of our teachers are great storytellers;

others use flannelgraphs well. Some are experts with visuals; some are good discussion leaders; and some rarely have classroom discipline problems. A coordinator of training can help teachers with specific needs by putting them in contact with other workers who have demonstrated competence in those areas. Teachers are capable of training teachers, but a systematic utilization of their strengths requires coordination.

The coordinator of training is not responsible for planning all training emphases. Individual program leaders should supervise the activities of their departments, including training opportunities. The role of the coordinator is to serve as an assistant (or resource person) to the leaders. He maintains the staff file that records: (1) the teacher's training involvement (books he has read, tapes he has listened to, classes he has observed, and workshops he has attended); and (2) the teacher's strengths (skills which she is willing to share with others).

A computer entry or record card for each teacher (active or former) is essential for the coordinator. As program leaders channel teacher information to him, he updates the file. As teachers request resource suggestions, he names which team members are competent to assist.

A coordinator of training will not make or break a Christian education program. However, a coordinated effort to match teacher strengths with other teacher needs is another way to maximize a church's training emphasis.

Conclusion

For years Redeemer Church struggled with its Sunday School. Student participation was sporadic, and teacher turnover was great. For a while it tried a bus ministry, but that eventually fizzled out. Sunday School contests would bring out some new children, but after the hype was over, so were the newcomers.

When Pastor Jensen came to Redeemer, he had a different strategy for the school. Numbers were not his primary concern. His desire was to see Redeemer offer the best Bible education in town. His commitment to a quality educational ministry necessitated some program and facility changes, but primarily his energy was channeled into developing a well-trained group of teaching ministers. Through proper recruitment, good team-building, and regular training, Bible-learning came alive in the congregation.

Today Redeemer Church is still struggling in its Sunday School, but the problem is different. Now there is a shortage of space because of all the new people who have come to the church. A competent teaching staff, excited about the Scriptures and their students, has produced what a dozen gimmicks could not generate. Pastor Jensen recognized that "any warm body won't do"—especially in the high task of communicating God's life-changing principles. And today the people at Redeemer share his vision and commitment.

A Checklist for Training

Does our church have . . .

☐ Meaningful Content

☐ A Variety of Formats

☐ High Expectations

☐ A Spirit of Camaraderie

☐ Sufficient Finances

☐ A Coordinator of Training

Sample Training Program

THE 5-50 PROTECTION PLAN
Five 50-minute sessions
throughout the 1990-91 **WHAT**
church year for Calvary's
Educational Ministers.

To **Strengthen and Enhance**
our various educational
ministries by providing our
personnel with stimulating **WHY**
opportunities for:
  ENCOURAGEMENT
  PROBLEM-SOLVING
  SKILL DEVELOPMENT

All ministry personnel are
invited:
  Sunday School/VBS Staff
  Club Workers/Youth Leaders **WHO**
  Children's Church Workers
  Interested Others

Sunday Mornings 8:35–9:25
  September 30
  November 18
  January 13 **WHEN**
  March 3
  April 21

CALVARY BAPTIST CHURCH **WHERE**
—Room Number 11—

Five-Fifty Training Program (Continued)

5-50 PROTECTION PLAN
1990–91 TOPICS

SEPTEMBER
Making the Environment Attractive

NOVEMBER
Using Curriculum Materials

JANUARY
Dealing with Difficult Students

MARCH
Promoting Student Involvement
and Participation by Asking the
Right Questions

APRIL
Telling Stories, Preparing Handouts,
and Using Visual Aids

Five-Fifty Training Program (Continued)

5-50 PROTECTION PLAN
for the
DEVELOPMENT of our MINISTRY PERSONNEL
1991–92 TOPICS

October 13
TEACHERS AND STUDENTS
"Building and Maintaining Relationships"

November 24
TEACHERS AND THE SUBJECT
"Encountering Christ and Making Him Live"

January 19
TEACHERS AND STUDY
"Developing Bible Study Skills
and Using Resource Materials"

March 8
TEACHERS AND SPIRITUAL GROWTH
"Developing Spiritual Disciplines
to Form Our Christian Character"

April 26
TEACHERS AND SOCIETY
"Training Our Students to Live for Christ"

"The attitudes and skills of our teachers
will make the difference
in the spiritual growth of our students"

—Craig Dahl
Session Facilitator

Used by permission of Calvary Church, Meriden, Connecticut.

Sample Training Program

SUPER SATURDAY
SEPTEMBER 6
8:30–3:00

We will be starting off this year with several hours of orientation, training, and planning. This is a *must* for all teaching staff. We will provide the continental breakfast and lunch for you.

All the teaching materials will be distributed and you will have several hours to plan with the others in your department. The new Sunday School year begins September 7.

Here's the schedule:

8:30–9:00	Continental Breakfast
9:00–9:30	Devotions/Prayer
9:30–10:15	Orientation to our methods of teaching "How do children learn?" Bible Learning Activities/ Guided Conversation
10:15–10:30	Break
10:30–11:30	Meet by age group—led by coordinators Orientation of materials Go through the schedule of the hour See introductory filmstrip
11:30–12:15	Session on Discipline
12:15–1:00	Lunch
1:00–3:00	Department Planning

Sample Training Program (Continued)

MONTHLY PLANNING/
TRAINING MEETINGS

We will do everything we can to make you successful as a Sunday School worker. At the monthly meetings you will receive training and make plans and pray together. *Attendance at these meetings is expected as part of your teaching commitment.* They are held at the church.

CHILDREN (grades 1–6)	EARLY CHILDHOOD (2–5-year-olds)
September 15	September 22
October 20	October 20
November 17	November 24
January 19	January 26
February 16	February 23
March 16	March 23
April 20	April 27
May 18	May 18

"Marvelous Mondays"

Used by permission of Grace Church of Edina, Minnesota.

CHAPTER FOUR

TEACHER BURNOUT AND TURNOVER

For the very first time John Larson had his Sunday School fully staffed. John had been the Sunday School superintendent for three years at Winfield Church. When he accepted the position he thought he'd have time to build and train the staff. Instead, it seemed like his job became nothing more than finding people to plug holes in the dike called Christian education.

Unfortunately, the month was April, and although the church had a full complement of teachers, John knew that by summer several people would relinquish their teaching assignments. As John reflected on his situation, he began to view staffing as a revolving door. In spite of all his efforts to shove people into the door, just as many seemed to fly out.

John's experience is not unique; it is shared by many pastors, superintendents, and program leaders. New teachers are hard enough to find, but leaders are even more disheartened when new recruits relinquish their assignments.

Interestingly, teacher turnover rates vary from congregation to congregation. While teacher burnout and turnover plagues some churches, others are relatively unaffected by the problem. The difference is related to a fundamental principle of staffing: the church that retains its staff has little or no need to find new staff.

Most people naively think that staffing is primarily an issue of recruitment (finding enough people to serve). However, the key issue in staffing is *retention,* keeping teachers motivated and satisfied with their teaching, so that they gladly serve year after year. Let me illustrate. At Jefferson Church the primary department is staffed by three people who have served together for eight years. At Evangel Church six couples have staffed the preschool departments for over fifteen years. The boys club at Bethlehem Temple is led by a team of men who have been together since the club's inception three years ago. The program leaders in these churches spend little time in recruitment because the retention of staff is very high.

When we think of teacher burnout and turnover, our focus is usually on the volunteer. But wait a minute! Let's look more carefully and ask a question. *Why* is that worker frustrated, overworked, or losing commitment? Maybe the problem does not solely lie with the teacher. Perhaps program leaders have contributed to the situation. Maybe the church is getting what it has paid for, reaping what it has sown.

A poor retention plan results in the need for a more intense recruitment plan. On the more positive side, the converse is also true. A good retention plan reduces the need for recruitment.

There are intentional things churches can do to build teacher motivation and help volunteers enjoy multiple years of service. As you evaluate your church's staffing retention plan, consider the importance of: proper recruitment; meaningful service; realistic tenures; available substitutes; team teaching; relevant training; regular communication; frequent encouragement; and helpful advocates.

Proper Recruitment
A good retention plan begins with proper recruitment (see Chapter 1). *A positive approach to recruitment* cultivates an atmosphere that esteems service. Programming is realistically staffable. Records are maintained for coordinating people's ministry. Genuine warmth, concern, and thoroughness characterize contacts with potential workers. Willing recruits are assisted with early training. And the whole recruitment endeavor is bathed in prayer.

A good recruitment plan also takes advantage of *a networking approach to staffing.* This strategy is very simple, yet many churches overlook its possibilities. Stated simply, staff programs with people who already have close ties. Folks who enjoy being with one another, are more likely to serve long-term together. An attempt to recruit three additional workers for the junior high department should include asking people who already "click" with those currently working with the teens. Their relationship is not only helpful in recruitment, but more important, it's a factor that will keep them working as a team over the long haul.

There are at least three networks to pursue in staffing. First, look for *natural friends* to work together in the Christian education program. The reason Faith Presbyterian's preschool department has been strong for ten years is because of the six couples (all at the same stage in life, and all natural friends) who serve together. While they primarily go to church on Sunday to teach, they also enjoy being with one another.

Second, consider *relatives* in a networking approach to staffing. While commitment levels, gifts and abilities vary, a family team approach has many advantages. Perhaps the greatest benefit is that the family members teach through their interaction, as well as through their instruction. In addition, working together in a specific ministry helps a family combat the pace and race which is tearing many apart. For example, in one club program, a father and his teenage son both work with younger boys. In another church, the children's coordinator recruits couples to staff programs.

Third, *new people to the church* serve as another network for staffing. While caution should be exercised in appointing new people too quickly, there is also a danger in keeping them too removed, waiting to prove themselves.

People can only sustain so many relationships, and older members already have their circle of friends. Consequently, new people can't crack into the circle. I frequently hear the statement: "I've been attending the church now for a year, and I still don't have any friends."

A good way to draw these folks in is by putting a few

together in several areas of service. There are many levels of involvement in a local church, and even relatively new people can assist in a club program, open their home for youth activities, or sing in the choir. The wise program leader will encourage newcomers to serve together in *ministry teams*.

Meaningful Service

People tend to avoid things they do poorly, yet eagerly involve themselves in discussions, sports activities, or tasks with which they feel comfortable. While some people may grudgingly agree to serve, it's the person who actually feels fulfilled in teaching, who will joyfully continue two, three, or even ten years.

When my children were toddlers they had a plastic toy into which they could place various shaped objects. The wedge, circle, oval, cross, square and rectangle were designed to fit through corresponding openings. Similarly, the program leader must also match people with proper ministry openings.

Sometimes staff shortages lead them to force some people into the wrong ministry slots. Unfortunately, this quick fix usually leads to long-term failure. However, when people are put into positions of service based on their gifts, desires, temperament, and background, they frequently enjoy a longer tenure of service. The word "joy" is significant. A teacher can usually tell if his service is meaningful by an inner assurance and contentment that what he is doing is correct. Proper recruitment and meaningful service are related, and together they reduce teacher turnover.

Realistic Tenures

Reasonable lengths of service encourage teacher commitment. Earlier we saw the value of using *appointments to service* for specifying the length of time a worker is expected to serve. These teacher contracts discourage turnover within the contractual period. A teacher who has agreed to work one year in the fours-and-fives department, for example will probably fulfill her commitment. At the end of the year teachers are given the choice of continuing in that class for another specified period, changing ministry areas, or taking a break from service. Churches that honor the requests of teachers build credibility with their volunteers and are more successful with subsequent recruitment efforts.

While I feel it is detrimental to use a monthly or quarterly tenure for service (see Chapter 1), there is value to *the three-one format*. Some churches find it easier to staff their Christian education programs by offering nine-month and three-month teacher contracts. A main group of workers is recruited to serve for the nine-month school year, while another team is built to work just for the summer months. In this three-one arrangement many of the regular staff are willing to serve year after year. For example, Blair and Pat King are public school teachers who work on Sundays in the toddler nursery at their church. Since school is out for the summer and their own children are grown, they like to travel from June to August. While most of the teachers at their church have accepted one-year contracts, Blair and Pat asked for the three-one arrangement. Since they were willing to work year after year, the Christian education committee gladly accommodated them.

Whether using the twelve-month contract, or the nine-month/three-month format, these longer tenures encourage ongoing service, more than a rotation or quarterly format. In addition, potential resentment is eliminated because teachers are assured that they will not be stuck in a situation indefinitely. If joy of service is lost, and a teacher has a chance to get out, she will not likely again be recruited for service. On the contrary, a realistic tenure of service, one that provides several months of ministry, but also offers a break in service, encourages teacher stability.

Available Substitutes

Within the contractual period, teachers may still need occasional breaks. Schedule conflicts, midyear vacations, or illnesses require the use of substitutes. An empathetic program leader who is willing to schedule substitutes cultivates appreciation and loyalty in the staff. These minibreaks also refresh workers for the long haul.

A program leader knows whether or not a teacher's request is valid. Teachers who are chronically absent need to be exhorted, but even the confrontation can be positive. "Fred, we've talked about your frequent need for substitutes in your fifth-grade class. I know you love the kids, but perhaps this is not a good time for you to be teaching. I'd love to have you on the teaching team, and I suggest you pray about whether you can finish this term, or if an appointment in another year might be better for your personal schedule." This approach is not a threat, but realistically helps the person assess whether or not he personally can handle his current commitment.

Some churches ask teachers to find their own substitutes. Unfortunately, this procedure lessens accountability to the superintendent, and permits a greater frequency of absenteeism. In fact, many superintendents do not know until an actual Sunday that their teacher will be absent. When program leaders assume responsibility for contacting substitutes, they keep abreast of what is happening within their departments. Furthermore, they can regulate how often particular substitutes are asked to serve.

Three good *sources for substitute teachers* are (1) people who have shown an interest in education, but have declined a teaching assignment; (2) professional school teachers; and (3) responsible youth and children.

The recruitment process normally uncovers *people who are open to the possibility of service,* but decide they cannot undertake the specific commitment. After graciously receiving their decline, a wise program leader will inquire whether they are willing to teach on a substitute basis. The frequency of subbing, the amount of lead time, and available materials should be clearly explained. When a person is assured that she'll not be asked more than once a month, he often will volunteer to serve as substitute.

(2) *Professional school educators* are also good resources for substitutes. Frequently school teachers are exhausted after a long week of teaching and are not eager to work with children again on Sundays. While some do help in Sunday School because they feel responsible to use their expertise, others pre-

fer a permanent ministry in another area of the church (like singing in the choir, or working on a committee). Many are also willing to work on a once-a-month basis as a substitute. Professional school teachers are usually flexible, needing less time for preparation. When there is a short notice for a substitute, a school teacher can move into the class situation more comfortably than a person who is unfamiliar with the teaching/learning process.

(3) A third source for substitutes is *responsible teens* and *children*. While I affirm the predominant usage of adults as teachers, a program leader should not overlook the service of young people to assist in children's ministry. In one church, for example, an eleven-year-old boy worked with his father in the three-year-old church time program. In a similar situation a nine-year-old girl assisted with the story time and table activity for kindergartners. Many churches have used teens to work alongside adults in the nursery.

I would not recommend using children where classes are self-contained (one teacher per room); young helpers need a competent adult with whom to work. But this practice has several benefits: adolescents are allowed to serve (all Christians need this to grow); children observe role models of older boys and girls; and the pool of potential substitutes is widened.

A growing number of churches are using *video cassettes as substitutes,* or for special programs, or during the summer. While this practice reduces the total number of staff needed for a program, it has several limitations. Videos actually reduce student involvement with both the lesson and each other. Videos may also weaken the shepherding ministry of the teacher. On the positive side, videotapes are good for a change of pace, and are helpful in short-term situations. As supplements of a competent teaching staff, videos can make a healthy contribution.

The good practice of having available substitutes will not in itself eliminate teacher burnout and turnover. But using people to step in and carry the load when time off is needed is part of an overall staffing game plan that tells teachers, "We understand, and we'll help you with your class this week." Since team spirit is part of building a long-tenured staff, then having available substitutes is an essential part of that process.

Team Teaching

It's easy to understand why Lucy Petersen feels the weight of her ministry. She has taught fourth-grade girls for three years in the bedroom of a home owned by the church. Each week she tells the Bible story, helps the students with their workbooks, and then draws them into a learning activity. Only Lucy knows what goes on behind her closed door, and rarely does anyone come in to help her, give her advice, or offer encouragement.

By contrast the Davises and Copelands work together in a third-and-fourth-grade department. These couples teach twenty-four children. They are crowded in their 600-square-foot room. Nevertheless, they manage well with three round tables for teaching centers. Sandy Davis works as the team leader, greeting children, taking attendance, and conducting their large-group times. Her husband and Ken and Jan Copeland each teach and shepherd a group of seven to nine children.

Each week the students enter their classroom and study with their regular teachers. Usually the Bible lesson is at tables, along with the workbook activity. Sometimes the whole class gathers together to sing songs or share what they have been learning. Other times the students move directly from their regular smaller group into learning activity groups. These Bible learning activities, planned at the monthly department meeting, offer the children a choice of three activities correlated with the lesson.

Team teaching heightens student interest and involvement, but equally important, it fosters staff camaraderie and accountability rarely available to the solo teacher. Each team member is needed, and one's very presence is an encouragement to the others. When one person is absent, the team can seek a substitute, or combine to cover for the missing member. Since they are all working together in the same room, all are aware of the problems and needs of students. For example, if Billy's behavior is disruptive, moving him to a different group within the same department may prove helpful.

When teachers feel isolated, they are more likely to get overwhelmed, without anyone knowing of their frustrations. Team teaching shares the weight of ministry over several shoulders within a department. In addition, the by-product of fellowship experienced by working together draws workers into longer service. People who enjoy one another and enjoy working together are usually willing to retain their ministry assignments.

Relevant Training

The importance of good training has been presented in the previous chapter, but its relationship to teacher turnover is also worth emphasizing. People who feel inadequate and incompetent, are rarely interested in multiple years of service. When people are naked, they want to hide, not be exposed. Good teacher training clothes people with the knowledge and skills necessary for confident teaching.

Training sessions must be meaningful, and they must offer variety in format. They should encourage total participation, demonstrate flexibility, and build a spirit of comaraderie. And they will need sufficient finances to make them top quality.

Both group training and individual assistance are beneficial to the novice. Observing good teaching models is helpful, and working alongside a lead teacher to improve on specific techniques is also productive. Relevant, meaningful training content will reduce teacher burnout.

Training helps people become more competent in what they do. When a worker senses an assurance that what she is doing is right and profitable, she also develops confidence. A competent and confident teacher is less likely to quit after her first appointment to service.

Regular Communication

Regular communication is necessary for developing a positive ministry atmosphere and therefore essential for long teacher tenures. Occasionally a worker will mention how an article mailed to the teachers was meaningful; it was the encouragement needed at that particular moment. This positive example reinforces the fact that good communication is profitable.

Negative experiences also illustrate the importance of good communication. We remember the teacher who was offended because he was not informed about a certain decision. It is not uncommon for program leaders to make changes in the time of Sunday School, the locations of classes, or even the curriculum, without asking for teacher input. A minimum courtesy is to let teachers at least know that those decisions are under review. A lack of open communication will lead some teachers to drop out, or maybe worse, keep them disgruntled and negative while still serving on the ministry team.

Let me encourage the use of two communication tools for developing a healthy team spirit. First, the *regular publications* of a church should frequently highlight educational ministries. Articles about specific programs inform workers about events taking place in each other's ministries. Good positive articles in a church newsletter, or on the back of a bulletin go beyond public relation purposes to the congregation as a whole. They also serve to bond together the teaching staff.

Second, *special mailings* to the educational faculty help teachers feel significant, and part of an important ministry team. For example, periodically I would mail *The Shepherd's Staff* to our workers (see samples at the end of this chapter). Six times a year the entire educational faculty would receive this letter, which included some personal thoughts, special happenings in our educational team, and reprints of practical articles. The content of the letter was helpful to our teachers, but even more valuable was the regular reminder that they were a team, the staff of the Chief Shepherd. Regular communication promotes camaraderie, which in turn strengthens a teacher's commitment to service.

Frequent Encouragement
Teachers appreciate an informative newsletter, or helpful article. But I have noticed greater responses of loyalty to me, the church, and a particular teaching assignment when I have taken time to encourage teachers personally. Frequent encour-

agement of teachers inspires retention of staff. I'm not suggesting a manipulative stroking of people, just to keep them serving. Flattery does not usually motivate people; instead, lack of sincerity turns people away. But honest appreciation should be expressed for a good attitude, or a job well done. Positive comments from parents should be passed on to teachers on a regular basis.

Frequent encouragement can take many forms. Some program leaders make phone calls just to find out how things are going and to share a word of thanks. Others use a written note to frame an uplifting thought. An occasional booklet with a personal note also demonstrates concern for the worker.

Timely words can cheer the spirit: "Frank, you look a little discouraged. Is there something troubling you that we can talk about?" The sincere words, "I'll pray for you," are reassuring to a teacher, especially when we inquire later as to how things turned out. An arm around the shoulder, a hug, or holding hands as we pray for one another or our students, also communicates caring. A teacher who feels valuable to a specific ministry is more likely to remain in that area of service.

A Helpful Advocate

Many teachers feel frustrated, and eventually give up teaching because they do not have someone to intercede for them regarding their needs. One teacher needs a larger classroom, another simply needs chalk for the chalkboard. Conflicts arise over materials that are always late, unrealistic teacher-student ratios, or simply a burned-out light that is not replaced. Countless "little foxes" rob our workers of the joy they deserve in their service.

When an education worker is recruited, and then stuck off in a corner to fend for herself, she begins to feel taken for granted. This attitude leads to a feeling of being used, then into bitterness and eventually into withdrawal. Once a teacher has mentally and emotionally relinquished her responsibility, she will soon leave the classroom.

A few gallons of paint are not that expensive; mounting a new blackboard is not that difficult. But the typical teacher does not usually have the clout to move the "powers that be" into action. Whether the teacher is facing poor acoustics, or a chronic student behavior problem, he needs someone to whom he can turn for assistance with his problem. The program leader must be the advocate to intercede for the staff. If he is not able to get action directly, he can take the request to his supervisor (the Sunday School superintendent, divisional leader, or pastor—depending on the size of the church) to see that the problem is resolved.

A helpful advocate is perceived by the teacher as more than just someone providing on-time materials; the leader is seen as someone genuinely concerned for the worker's welfare. Again, a teacher who feels cared for, is more likely to serve over the long haul.

Conclusion

Why is it that one church in a particular town has an annual teacher turnover rate of 75 percent, while a similar church across town (same denomination and size) has a turnover rate of less than 5 percent? It's not an issue of luck; nor is it an issue of one group being more spiritual. The reason Lakeside Church has long teacher tenures is that its leaders work hard at a comprehensive retention plan.

None of the nine principles studied in this chapter will independently eliminate teacher burnout and turnover. Proper recruitment, but no training, hinders retention. Frequent encouragement of teachers, but not providing them with substitutes, or interceding for them when they have a need, seems shallow and insincere. But when a church's staffing plan includes all of these principles, teachers will experience joy in their service and a closeness in their team relationships. Teachers who find fulfillment in their ministries, will likely retain their positions for many years.

A Checklist for Retention

Does our church have . . .

☐ Proper Recruitment

☐ Meaningful Service

☐ Realistic Tenures

☐ Available Substitutes

☐ Team Teaching

☐ Relevant Training

☐ Regular Communication

☐ Frequent Encouragement

☐ Helpful Advocates

Sample Staff Communique
The Shepherd's Staff
Trinity Church, 2130 E. University Drive, Mesa, AZ 85203

March 1, 1979

Dear Education Worker:

This is the second issue of the *Shepherd's Staff,* Trinity's bi-monthly educational faculty communique. We who are the Shepherd's staff have much to be thankful and much to praise God for in these early months of 1979. Although many times we tend to look at a problem in our program, such as the need for another worker, the bus that fails to start, or whatever else is your personal thorn in the flesh, a broader look would reveal there are many things that we can be thankful for. Let me list just a few:

*record high attendances in Sunday School, the highest being 678 this month
*Awana clubs pulling near the 200 mark in clubbers
*good reports on the Women's Ministries Bible Studies
*significant praise to God for personal growth through our growth group program
*a new desire on the part of many of our adult classes to be a base for ministry
*the early plans to have Dr. Launstein as our Family Camp speaker, and Harold Westling for our men's retreat.
*AND THE MOST EXCITING—the arrival of Dan and Lee Rachoy next month to coordinate our Christian Education Ministries.

1978 has been a year of numerical as well as personal growth. I am personally looking forward to Dan's arrival, for the coordination, staffing, and training essential for our ministry necessitates a full-time person who can work with us individually and as team members of specific programs.

79

Since some of you have young children, you are aware that I offered to the parents who received the *Family Letter,* the book *You Can Be Your Own Child's Counselor* by Elizabeth Skoglund. Since this book deals with self-esteem, building trust, communication, and other child-related concerns, I would like to make this book available to you also to strengthen your ministry. If you desire a free copy of this good book on child development, please see me at the office.

Many of you have shared concerns regarding classroom management. I have a number of good tapes and books, as well as articles on the subject of discipline and classroom control. If you desire some of this information, please take the time to see me for it. Proper classroom control is essential to maintain a good learning atmosphere for your children, as well as to maintain sanity for yourself.

Lastly, let me mention that I have placed on the back of this page several factors which research has found to be successful in motivating children who lack motivation. Perhaps you can think of a specific child or young person in your ministry who seems to lack a desire to be involved and grow. Try one or two of the items listed on the back side as specific work projects with that child.

Your Co-Worker in Christ,

Pastor John Cionca

Sample Staff Communique
The Shepherd's Staff

Trinity Church, 2130 E. University Drive, Mesa, AZ 85203

July 1, 1979

Dear Christian Worker:

The last issue of *The Shepherd's Staff* came to you in May when school was still in session. It seems hard to believe that already we are nearing the middle of the summer, and that before we know it, the cool temperatures of the fall will be upon us (I know this is hard for some to believe!). This issue of *The Shepherd's Staff* will not be heavy. Our desire this month is to share with you an article by G. Weatherley on teacher's preparation, and to share with you a poem which illustrates the seriousness of the task that is before us. Let's consider each of our students in light of the description below:

I took a piece of plastic clay
And idly fashioned it one day.
And as my fingers pressed it still
It bent and yielded to my will.
I came again when days had passed,
That lump of clay was hard at last,
The form I gave it, still it bore,
But I could change it nevermore.

I took a child, God's living clay,
And gently shaped it day by day
And molded with my Saviour's art
A young child's soft and yielding heart.
I came again when years were gone.
He was a man I looked upon.
But still that early image bore,
But I could change him nevermore.

—Author unknown

Although this may sound a little overdone, let us say that we are sincerely proud of each one of you. By your willingness to serve, you are following the example of Christ and His design for your spiritual growth. Pray with us that others will also see the joy there is in investing one's life for others.

Your Co-Workers in Christ,

Dan and John

CHAPTER FIVE

LACK OF BIBLE MEMORIZATION

For God so loved the world that He . . ." If you are a typical church leader, you are able to complete that statement. Why? Because you have memorized John 3:16. Perhaps like Timothy you have been instructed in the Scriptures from childhood. Christians view the Bible as a friend that gives counsel; a navigational instrument that directs their journey; a playbook that diagrams how the game of life should be executed. Scriptures committed to memory are used daily by the Holy Spirit to speak and direct our lives.

But wait a minute! If Scripture memorization is so important, why do pastors list lack of Bible memorization among their top five Christian education problems? Are Christians memorizing Scripture less today?

The feeling among many ministers is that adults are memorizing less today than they have in the past. When they were children parents helped them with memory work. Time was made for recitation of verses, and they were frequently rewarded for their efforts. But *adults are not forced* to do memory work, so many no longer systematically study this way.

Many children are memorizing less Scripture today than their counterparts did two decades ago. Churches have seen *a proliferation of educational and musical programs, and more sophisticated learning techniques.* Colorful curriculum, audiovisuals, and well-equipped rooms, have replaced simple lessons.

Instead of a flannelgraph presentation followed by rote recitation, modern curriculum employs scores of Bible-learning activities to teach the theme of a passage.

The proliferation of Bible translations has further complicated the memorization of Scripture. When many of us were children, there were two prominent translations, with some newcomers penetrating the field. Today there are scores of translations, five even having their own complete concordances (KJV, RSV, TLB, NASB, NIV). The lack of a common Bible version discourages group reading and recitation. When people don't practice memory work together, they lose the motivational benefit of accountability.

The pace and race of daily schedules also squeezes out Bible memory. Unfortunately, many families are sacrificing the important for the urgent. While Dad's schedule has increased some, Mom's schedule and that of the kids has skyrocketed. More than 60 percent of married women work outside (*and* inside) the home. Children now participate in community cultural activities, art activities, and athletic programs.

Our educational sophistication, proliferation of translations, and fast-paced living have not been a calculated attack on Bible memory; nevertheless, their subliminal impact is significant.

Can we as church leaders reverse this trend? Can Bible memorization become a regular feature of our church programming? Can our members again emphasize it as a personal spiritual discipline? The answer to these questions is a resounding yes. The proof lies in the fact that many individuals and congregations are having good success in this area. But before I share several suggestions, let me first articulate four assumptions worth clarifying regarding memorization.

Assumptions about Memorization

My first assumption is that *memorization is important.* While this statement seems obvious, some challenge it openly, while others indirectly deny it through their indifference.

Why don't you memorize the telephone numbers of all your friends? You might respond, "Why bother, the numbers are at my fingertips if I need them." Some individuals feel the same way about memorization. Having a Bible close at hand, and being familiar with its content is valuable, but some feel to actually memorize it is more work than it's worth.

But there's a danger in that attitude. For example, while an astronaut might take his flight manual into space, he still memorizes hundreds of procedures essential to his well-being. Similarly, having the Lord's precepts stored for immediate recall is important for daily living. In the words of Moses, the Scriptures "are not just idle words for you—they are your life" (Deut. 32:47).

Psalm 119:11 states: "I have hidden Your word in my heart *that* I might not sin against You" (emphasis mine). Notice the time reference. The Psalmist had stored the Lord's commands in his intellect and affections so that when he was tempted to sin, the words would direct him away from disobedience. The Bible is not simply a manual that can be consulted periodically; it is a book of living words that gives insight for godly living.

I offer the second assumption as a caution that *memorization does not equal spirituality*. While it is desirable to program our minds with God's living Word, we cannot assume that knowledge of the Scriptures (or even memorization) assures godly maturity. We are all familiar with individuals who are walking encyclopedias of Bible knowledge, yet are insensitive, proud, or even caustic.

The child who has memorized 300 verses does not automatically become less self-centered than the child who learned only ten verses. It may only demonstrate he was more highly motivated to perform a given task for the reward he would get. While I do believe there is a correlation between a sincere commitment to memorization and spiritual growth, it's naive to think that the practice alone produces maturity.

My third assumption deals with the purpose of memory work: *memorization is not an end process, but paves the way for ongoing meditation*. The Apostle Paul instructs Christians to put off the old self and put on the new self. He tells them that this is accomplished "by the renewing of your mind" (see Rom. 12:2; Eph. 4:22-24). A Christian's attitudes, speech, and actions can find direction each day from a mindset that is God-centered. His desire is to "practice the presence of Christ."

Since God's thoughts are higher than our thoughts and His ways higher than our ways (Isa. 55:8-9); our computer brains are programmed best with His viewpoint. God's values are revealed primarily in the Scriptures. As we store His Word in our hearts, the Holy Spirit brings those verses to memory at appropriate times. For example, when I'm tempted to yell at my children, a bell goes off in my mind: "A gentle answer turns away wrath, but a harsh word stirs up anger" (Prov. 15:1). When I feel ripped off, the bell goes off again: "Love . . . keeps no record of wrongs" (1 Cor. 13:4-5). The point of this discipline is not to display a trophy that says I have memorized a thousand verses. It is to foster meditation and application of the Scripture in my daily walk.

My fourth assumption is related to learning theory: *memorization that is meaningful is best caught, not taught.* Parents who harp on their children Sunday morning to learn their memory verses, but do not exemplify memorizing Scripture themselves are saying one thing verbally, but experientially teaching the opposite. While children do learn verses because of pressure or reward, secondary reinforcements will not produce an ongoing lifestyle of memorization.

By way of contrast, parents who intentionally allow their children to observe them memorizing, are in a better position to pass on this discipline. Handing your Bible to a child while you state, "Hey, Ben, check me on these verses," is a teaching vehicle too infrequently used by parents.

With these assumptions now stated, let me list a number of suggestions that will help churches encourage better memorization. Bible memorization will increase when a church: stresses the value of memorization; uses a preferred translation; provides a program with accountability; offers helps for memorization; and takes advantage of short-term approaches to memorization.

Stress the Value of Memorization
Many Bible passages stress the importance of meditating on Scripture. Joshua 1 records the promise of success for those

who meditate on God's Law. Psalm 119 explains that hiding the Scriptures in one's heart leads to a godly walk. Second Timothy 3 reveals that the Bible is profitable to teach and train, and also to correct and rebuke.

The value of memorization is best demonstrated by the Lord Jesus. When tempted by the devil, he responded by quoting the Scriptures. If Jesus took the time to learn the Scriptures to the point where he could quote them, then His disciples will profit by following His example.

People's beliefs are reflected by what they say, but their values are revealed by what they actually do. A congregation will not develop a high view of memorization merely by a pastor exhorting them to learn the Word. Just as Christ demonstrated Scripture memory, *church leaders can exemplify* a commitment to storing significant verses in their minds. The pastor in his sermons can quote an occasional verse as he explains the Scriptures. The Sunday School teacher, club worker, or youth sponsor can insert a memorized verse or two that was personally meaningful. Bible quotations can serve to introduce hymns. Even games can be played where verses are begun and the class (or congregation) is asked to complete the quotation.

Some churches have stressed the importance of memorization by selecting a theme verse each year and *a key verse each month*. While different age groups memorize verses in their respective programs, the congregation as a whole also learns the key verse together. Some churches print the verse in their newsletter and on their bulletin each Sunday of the month. Some have even taken time in a worship service to recite together the verse of study.

Presenting gifts that encourage memorization is another way to elevate the value of memory work. Graduation is a special time in the life of a high school senior. One church typically gave a subscription for a collegiate magazine to their graduates, but recently changed the practice. They now give a graduation gift of the *NIV Navigators Topical Memory System* to their graduates.

Many churches follow a long-term practice of *awarding*

87

camp scholarships for memory work. This too places value on memorization. Churches that are successful in this endeavor publicize the program well in advance. Some give camp dollars for individual passages, while others knock off a certain portion of the camp fee, or cover the entire fee if a child completes the program. Size and difficulty of portions are selected in accord with the conceptual learning stage of the child. For example, one church uses key doctrinal verses for their high schoolers to memorize. The particulars of these programs vary from church to church, but the practice of Scripture memory for camp attendance helps students both study the Word and participate in a great learning environment.

Use a Preferred Translation

Another suggestion that will help churches in memorization is to adopt a common Bible translation. I know what you're thinking: easier said than done! I agree. While some people prefer ham on rye to salami on pumpernickel, so some people prefer the NASB to the NIV. Furthermore, just as some people insist that the reuben is the only way to go, so a number will insist that only the King James is inerrant. Nevertheless, preaching is more easily followed when the congregation uses a similar translation, and so is memorization easier when one translation is predominantly utilized.

Though church leaders cannot legislate which translations people use, they can make it convenient for people to use a common translation. Andover Church made purchasing new Bibles for the sanctuary their Thanksgiving project. They placed in each pew a modern translation which already had broad appeal in the congregation, and from which the pastor preached.

Franklin Chapel purchased, at a discount price, a large shipment of Bibles in the translation they endorsed. These were acquired in November, and it was suggested that people buy copies to give as Christmas gifts to family members and friends.

Many churches award Bibles to their children, usually as promotion gifts when they reach a certain grade level.

Churches that follow this practice should not look for the least expensive Bibles, but for a children's edition of the translation used by the leadership and church body.

Using a common version makes it possible for students in class to memorize directly from the Scripture, and not just from activity pages or workbooks. A common text can help two people memorize together, or even a group of individuals learn a given passage. Adopting a preferred translation will not in itself assure a memorizing congregation, but it will remove one of the barriers that hinders group memorization.

Provide a Program with Accountability

When a person is born into the family of God, he becomes a Christian. Instantly he has many spiritual brothers and sisters. God has not called His adopted children to fend for themselves (see Heb. 10:24-25). While Christians can individually memorize important Bible verses, frequently they need the encouragement of another person to help them continue the practice. Therefore, it is beneficial for churches to provide a program that uses accountability to encourage memorization.

Many congregations entrust memorization to the Sunday School, while others assign it to the club program. Unfortunately, a closer investigation sometimes reveals that neither program is accomplishing the task. Let me illustrate. At Marquette Church several Sunday school teachers assumed that the Wednesday night staff stressed memorization, while the club workers thought the Sunday School teachers did it. In actuality, very few teachers were requiring memorization, and none of the adult programs encouraged it.

Assurance that Bible memorization is taking place somewhere in the church begins with the Christian Education Committee determining which program per age group is best suited to oversee the memory work. Supervision is then needed to help ministries achieve their goals and guide other programs away from duplication. For example, if a church is using its midweek club program for Bible memorization, then leaders should make sure the Sunday School teachers do not assign large portions for memory.

Relatively few adult Sunday School classes encourage memorization. But many churches are successful in helping adults memorize through home Bible studies. The smaller cell group makes the assigning of verses and the recitation of verses more feasible. For example, the adults in the home Bible study program at Southside Church learn twenty-six verses in their first nine-month period together. Those that continue on in other groups memorize additional verses.

Memorization in the youth ministry is similar to that of the adult ministry. A vehicle for accountability is essential, and several churches have chosen the midweek discipleship group as the place for some memory work. Sure we'd like all our youth to memorize the Scripture, but a large group meeting like the Sunday School, where there is a greater variety of commitment levels, is not a place of high accountability.

Most children's programs have enough subdivisions that at some place in the program a small enough teacher-student ratio exists for a teacher to work on Bible memorization. Some students require only a simple smile or hug from their teachers after they have completed a memory verse to keep them going week after week. Others need the motivation of a chart and the privilege of putting a star after each verse they complete. Some children thrive under a club program that offers ranks, badges, and numbers indicating student point achievements; for others this competitiveness is a turnoff.

Whatever the format, an ongoing system of accountability is another factor that encourages both the memorization and application of Scripture.

Offer Helps for Memorization

Churches that are serious about Bible memorization frequently provide resources that facilitate memory work. For example, the teachers at Kenwood Church handletter weekly verses for their children on colorful card stock. At St. Paul's Church the youth director provides a blue notebook for the teens in his discipleship group. In addition to their Bible study work, these young people write out the verses which they are trying to memorize. The men's early morning study at Central

Church uses 3″ x 5″ cards to record the verses their group is working on. In each of these churches the leadership has gone beyond merely suggesting texts to memorize; they have also provided resources (notebooks, packets of cards) to help their learners.

Things quickly memorized can just as quickly be forgotten. But things mastery-learned over time, will remain with us long-term. A personal record system of verses, therefore, further facilitates memorization. For example, some people use colored pencils to highlight verses in their Bibles and memorize directly from the texts. As they reread their Bibles, the marked verses are easily reviewed.

Many teens and adults have profited from the *Navigators Topical Memory System*. Packets of cards on salvation, temptation, victory, etc., are available in several translations. Blank cards are also available for recording other verses worth memorizing. The Navigators also market a wooden box for filing verse cards. When verses are stored by themes, groups of references can be easily retrieved and reviewed.

The degree of commitment to a system, and the amount of time spent in reviewing verses will vary among people. But any system that highlights significant verses will enhance better habits of Scripture memorization.

Advantages of Short-Term Approaches to Memorization

A few years ago I invited several of my neighbors to join in a neighborhood Bible study. My plan was to spend Thursday evenings during the school year studying the Book of Acts. One neighbor expressed that he couldn't afford to invest that much time, but if I could offer a six-week study he would come.

Tom's hesitancy to commit himself to a long-term project is shared by many people. While some individuals will get involved in a club program, discipleship group, or home Bible study, others will only make a short-term commitment. The challenge to memorize a shorter passage of Scripture at key times throughout the year may attract these individuals.

For example, there are specific events on a church calendar useful for a periodic all-church memorization effort. During the Advent or Lenten seasons, a portion of Scripture reproduced in the bulletin can bring together memorization emphasis. Similarly, a portion on freedom (e.g., Gal. 5:1, 16-18) is appropriate for the Fourth of July. Portions on outreach or witness (e.g., Rom. 10:9-15) fit well into a missions conference.

A number of congregations use the summer months to emphasize memorization. In an attempt to vary their Wednesday evening format, East Essex Church pairs their adults to memorize a verse from which the pastor will bring a meditation. Greenbrier Fellowship uses the children's Sunday School hour for additional memory work during July. Parklawn Church offered a summer adult elective class which consisted only of memorization and recitation of Scripture. Each of these short-term endeavors helped some people get involved in memorization for the very first time.

One last means of memorization is worth mentioning. Many people listen to music for pleasure and relaxation, but music is also profitable for worship and instruction. Have you noticed how the jingles on television commercials are easily memorized? Many Christian song writers are using the same phenomenon to record Scripture in song. Whether it be the *Kids Praise* albums or many of the praise choruses, music is an uplifting way to treasure God's eternal message in our hearts.

Conclusion

Back in the 1970s I spent six years working through a Ph.D. program. The rigors of papers, tests, comprehensive exams, dissertation, and oral defense did not keep me from finishing that program. However, a year after I graduated, I enrolled in a simple correspondence course but failed to complete the work. What was the difference? The formal schooling forced deadlines, dates and standards upon me; the correspondence course left me on my own. The press of a busy schedule crowded out my independent studies. In a similar way, many people recognize the importance of memorizing Scripture, but they let life's demands drain their daily time and energy.

Bible memorization is hard work. It's easier to sit in front of the television drinking a Coke and eating pretzels than to tax oneself learning the Scriptures. In fact, it's even easier to spend physical energy in a work project than to spend mental energy concentrating on a Bible text. Nevertheless, if we value the meditation of relevant Scripture at critical moments in our day, then we must work hard at producing an atmosphere that encourages the memorization of Scripture in our churches. Common translations, ongoing programs with accountability, short-term approaches, and helps for memorization will all facilitate better Bible knowledge.

A Checklist for Bible Memorization

Does our church . . .

☐ Stress the Value of Memorization

☐ Designate a Preferred Translation

☐ Provide a Program with Accountability

☐ Offer Helps for Memorization

☐ Take Advantage of Short-Term Approaches to Memorization

Example of a Short-Term
Approach to Memorization

WATER OLYMPICS
1. The Libya Launch
2. The Bay of Pigs
3. Lebanon Cup
4. Canoe Race
5. Frog Jump

FIELD OLYMPICS
1. The Yokes on You
2. Rock-putt
3. Frisbee Fling
4. Soccer-Rocker
5. Great Relay

POINTS: 1st 10,000
2nd 7,000
3rd 5,000
4th 3,000

WEEKEND TEAM COMPETITION

Ping Pong......... 1,000
Volleyball.......... 5,000
Basketball......... 5,000
Softball 5,000
Soccer............ 5,000
Horsehoes......... 1,000
Fishing Contest 10,000
Team Hymn Sing .. 10,000
Saturday Night Alive 5,000

Table Games 1,000
Canoe Races 1,000
Jigsaw Puzzles 5,000
Tennis (singles or doubles)
.... 1,000
Scripture Memory (Psalm 42)............. 20,000
Any other approved competition?
Treasure Hunt .. 100 points per item
Walking .. 1,000 points per mile

Each year the Family Camp of Colony Park Church, Edina, Minnesota divides its members into teams for some enjoyable competition. Notice from the Schedule of Events the high value placed on Bible memorization. Of the 23 people that memorized all of Psalm 42, the youngest was 8, and the oldest 72.

Scripture Memory Programs for Children

AWANA Youth Association
International Headquarters
3201 Tollview Drive
Rolling Meadows, IL 60008
(708) 394-5150

Bible Quiz Guidelines
Evangelical Free Church of America
1515 East 66th Street
Richfield, MN 55423
(612) 866-3343

Christian Service Brigade
P.O. Box 150
Wheaton, IL 60189
(708) 665-0630

Pioneer Clubs
P.O. Box 788
Wheaton, IL 60189
(708) 293-1600

Scripture Memory Fellowship International
P.O. Box 2455
St. Louis, MO 63141
(314) 569-0244

Well-Versed Kids
NavPress
P.O. Box 20
Colorado Springs, CO 80901

CHAPTER SIX

APATHY AND DECLINING ATTENDANCE

It's time for a faithfulness quiz. Which of the following statements is true?

A. People are less religious than they were a decade ago.

B. Church membership is on the decline.

C. Sunday School attendance is decreasing.

D. There's a growing disinterest among adults regarding Bible study.

E. All of the above.

The answer to this question is largely colored by the filters of your own congregation. According to recent Gallup Polls, a growing number of Americans have expressed belief in God. Furthermore, since 1970 church membership has increased 6 percent. And in the last decade there has been an explosion in Bible study materials, for both church and parachurch organizations are promoting adult study groups. Since the answer to my question can't be "E" (All of the above), that leaves "C" to be the true statement: there is a continual decrease in Sunday School attendance among Protestant denominations.

A few years ago I came across some interesting statistics. Out of forty-two Protestant denominations that were studied, twenty-four reported church growth, but only nine indicated that their Sunday Schools had grown. In fact, only three of the forty-two denominations could report a growth of over 1 percent in the church school. It is not surprising, therefore, that pastors I have surveyed reported apathy and declining attendance as a significant educational problem in the church.

Some congregations are experiencing decline in their Sunday Schools, but growth in their cell group ministries. Other churches are struggling with apathy and decline in all of their programs. My purpose in this chapter is not to promote one approach over another, but to present several principles that will build enthusiasm in any program. These factors are applicable to the morning worship service, Sunday School, home Bible study, or children's choir. They are principles that deal with attitudes and quality of program. They are commonsense suggestions that eat away at the underlying causes of apathy. The presence or absence of these qualities can be seen quickly when visiting a church.

A Tale of Two Churches

When I moved from the pastorate to the seminary, our family looked for a new church home. For several months we visited many congregations. Each Sunday we would talk together about our experience, specifically asking the children for their input. Sometimes the children would complain, "I don't like this church, Dad." Other times they would exclaim, "Let's join this place; I like it here!" Interestingly, their observations about their Sunday School classes usually paralleled my wife's and my observations about our class. Make your own observations as I tell you about two particular adult classes.

When my wife and I arrived at Church A, we asked some folks where we could attend Sunday School. No one knew where the class for our age group was meeting. We finally located the class, at 9:45 A.M., but there were only two people in the room. Since they were engaged in conversation, we just sat down at one of the tables. Eventually people trickled in and after about fifteen minutes things got underway.

The announcement time was first, and for ten minutes a missions committee representative tried to solicit volunteers to decorate the sanctuary for the upcoming missions conference. The pastor wanted each class to make a banner. Since there were no takers, a task force was appointed to bring a suggestion to the next class meeting.

Next the teacher began his lesson by trying to extricate himself from a theological mistake he apparently had made the previous Sunday. Rather than just recognizing the error, or getting on to the current lesson, he spent ten more minutes explaining why he had come to that poor conclusion.

During the middle of his defense, two women came in with refreshments and began to distribute forks, napkins, cake, and coffee. At this point the teacher was upstaged. Eventually order was restored, and the day's lesson began.

At 10:26 A.M. the teacher started reading Job, chapter 17, interspersing three or four extemporaneous comments on the text. Twelve minutes later he finished the chapter, looked at his watch, and concluded: "Well, we only have seven minutes left, and since that's not enough time to do chapter eighteen, let's just close in prayer." After exchanging a few pleasantries, my wife and I found our children, and moved into the sanctuary for the worship service.

A few weeks later we visited Church B. This church had greeters in the hallway, and although the couple did not know the location of my daughter's room, the wife inquired at the church office, and then cheerfully escorted Ben and Betsy to their classrooms. Meanwhile, her husband introduced us to a couple who took us to our adult class.

As we entered the classroom, several friendly people greeted us. Each was wearing a name tag, and there were blank name tags for visitors. After the class leader greeted us, one couple invited us to have a cup of coffee with them at their table. Shortly thereafter, the leader moved to the front of the room, made several pertinent announcements, and then introduced us to the whole class.

The teacher began his lesson by asking a question, and instructing each table to discuss it among themselves. After making some general comments about the role of Israel's prophets, he directed each table to answer a series of questions from the Minor Prophet assigned to them.

After twenty minutes in our smaller groups, he drew us

back together with a mini-lecture. Next, a representative from each table shared the results of their study. The leader summarized the lesson theme with suggestions for personal application. We concluded in small-group prayer around the tables.

Now let me ask a simple question: Which church would you like to attend week after week? Let me raise another question related to apathy and declining attendance: To which congregation would you prefer to bring a visitor? The answer to both questions is obvious.

Any church can turn apathy and decline into enthusiasm and growth by developing: a positive self-image; a format that recognizes differences; a competent teaching staff; relevant topics of study; methodologies that encourage involvement; a warm learning environment; room for growth; sufficient financial resources; and a marketplace mentality.

A Positive Self-Image

You only have to visit a church once to pick up vibrations on how the church feels about itself. Some churches communicate, "Why are you visiting us? We're just a poor, struggling congregation with some real problems." While other churches communicate, "We're a great church, and we know you'll eventually join our congregation if you visit a few times."

A church's self-image develops over time and is related to a number of factors. However, there is also a certain mystery about self-image. We are not always aware of influences which have shaped it. The situation is comparable to a couple adults similar in appearance, age, intelligence, and vocation, yet greatly different internally. One exudes a good self-understanding and appreciation, while the other reveals self-doubt and feelings of inferiority. This contrast displays itself even in the attitudes of children. One child despairs, "I can't do it"; the other asks, "Why don't you let me try?" A newcomer to the congregation can quickly figure out whether a church basically feels negative or positive about itself.

The visitor's first impression begins as he drives onto the church campus. A well-planned, carefully maintained *facility* communicates a positive message. I'm not advocating stained-glass windows, and fourteen-karat doorknobs. Rather it is a composite of little things that reveals members' feelings about their church. Healthy pride is visible in sharp pencils in the pew rack, a good supply of registration cards or offering envelopes, hymnals placed in the same direction, directories or signs in the hallways, clean restrooms, clean walls and windows, adequate lighting and ventilation, and neat grounds.

Let me illustrate. I visited a suburban church where the paint was peeling on the exterior walls of two of its three buildings. The carpeting in the narthex was torn, and handprints were in abundance on the walls of the hallway. Their problem wasn't lack of money but a lack of pride and commitment to their church.

By contrast I attended another church and was pleasantly surprised to see decorations in the foyer, a candle in each window, and the church dressed up with greens. My first impression was that these people really enjoy their church, and their worship service confirmed that fact for me.

Self-image is also communicated through *interpersonal relationships.* How people treat the newcomer is obviously important; but how they interact with one another is equally significant. Do people praise and encourage one another, or do they talk negatively or cut one another down (even in jest)?

Self-image is related to *personal involvement.* Do the people really sing during the hymns? Do they use their Bibles during the sermon? Are they eager to serve? Are they regular in attendance?

Another indicator of self-image is a church's *generosity.* Do they recognize the dedication of the church organist, grant a brief sabbatical to the pastor, or make an annual contribution to the police and fire departments (since churches are not taxed, yet still receive their services)? People who demonstrate generosity are usually people who feel good about themselves. This same principle applies to congregational life.

By now some of you may be asking, "Our church doesn't have a good self-image, so what can we do?" Learning theorists explain that people will live up to our expectations. They also believe that "as we think, we will do." Furthermore, "as we do, so we will think." Both are true.

A church that is experiencing apathy can reverse the attitudes and behaviors. First, the pastor and leaders must renew their understanding of the greatness of God and rekindle their passion for His church. Second, each small, positive step (in attitude or deed) should be praised. Healthy attitudes stimulate positive behavior, and healthy service stimulates positive attitudes. Perhaps one or two people will commit themselves to maintain the lawn and shrubbery. Maybe one person will volunteer to collect clothing for a nearby shelter. Every step in the direction of improving the quality of plant, praise, program, or outreach will further encourage a positive self-image.

A Format That Recognizes Differences

Since people are different, a church will reach a larger constituency through a variety of educational emphases. These specialized ministries include programs for mothers of preschoolers, single parents, families with Downs Syndrome children, businessmen, artists, sports enthusiasts, those fighting weight problems, and the list goes on. A church builds enthusiasm for its program by observing things that people are already interested in and excited about and then showing how Christ is relevant in those areas.

A format that recognizes differences offers a *diversity of program*. It will recognize that some people prefer a cottage prayer meeting to a centralized midweek service. It will realize that mothers at home would enjoy a mother's day out. It understands that women employed outside of the home cannot attend a morning Bible study, so it provides an evening Bible fellowship.

An insightful church knows that children need changes of pace in their program, rather than a passive impressional program. It empathizes with seniors who prefer a daytime fellowship over going out at night or in the cold.

A format that recognizes differences not only offers a diversity of program, but also provides *diversity within a program*. For instance, not all fourth-graders are alike. A nine-year-old can have a reading level anywhere from first grade to ninth grade, and his maturity level, desires and skills equally vary. Adults also differ from one another and bring a rich background of experience to each session. The teacher using only one or two classroom methods is less effective than the teacher who provides a choice of activities for the students. A variety of educational emphases will produce enthusiasm, because it recognizes individual differences.

A Competent Teaching Staff

Only the most deeply committed adults (or most foolish) will keep attending a Bible class taught by an incompetent teacher. If a situation like this is ongoing, the members are probably attending for a reason other than study (usually the fellowship of their peers). Though children and teens are sometimes forced to attend similar programs, if the choice were theirs, they would rather bail out. An effective teaching staff is one of the essential links in the chain of new enthusiasm and growth.

A competent teacher obviously must *understand the subject matter.* Whether the lesson is from the Old Testament or New Testament, from narrative or teaching passages, the good teacher must understand what the text means. He doesn't need a seminary degree, but he must do his homework to explain a given Scripture portion.

Furthermore, the competent teacher must *understand the teaching-learning process.* Just because a teacher is moving her lips does not mean that learning is taking place. The effective teacher mixes an understanding of her students with her knowledge. Furthermore, she uses appropriate methodology to bridge her knowledge to the students' understanding.

The "community of faith" model of education reminds us that the competent teacher also lives his *life as an example* before his students. A teacher who is authentic and demonstrates genuine concern builds a rapport that helps students more appreciate the teacher's instruction. Contacts that are made with students outside of the learning session build positive attitudes about the class itself. Anything that will improve the character or skills of teachers will result in greater interest on the part of the students.

Relevant Topics of Study

What are you studying in Sunday School next quarter? Some may respond, "Whatever the publishing house sends us." Others will answer, "Whatever the teachers choose to teach." The curriculum itself will not make or break a class. Even with poor curriculum, a good teacher can manipulate the learning environment to make a lesson interesting. Other dynamics in the classroom, including friendliness and fellowship, can keep a class going.

Selecting the best curriculum, however, and orchestrating it with other learning factors produces an exciting combination. Good curriculum is biblical, attractive, and methodologically sound. But relevancy is key to drawing people. The greater the relevancy of a topic to the learner's life situation, the more likely he is to participate. In a course on "The Christian and Personal Finance," for example, the young marrieds class could give extra emphasis to budgeting, while the seniors class could include an emphasis on investments or living trusts.

Irrelevant Sunday School classes produce apathy, which in turn leads to decline in attendance. Relevant topics of study foster enthusiasm, which in turn produces growth.

Methodologies That Encourage Involvement

Teaching methodologies that encourage involvement draw learners into the educational process. Long lectures (with adults) or long stories (with children) do not help students develop their own study skills. However, asking Scripture-search questions (with adults or youth), or unscrambling a Bible verse (with children or youth) *enhances learning.*

Three days after a learning experience people retain only 10 percent of what they hear, and 20 percent of what they see. But they will remember 65 percent of what they see and hear, and 90 percent of what they actually do with their hands. I, personally, cannot understand why a teacher would spend hours in study and preparation and then present the lesson with a method that restricts learning. Teachers who invest precious time in preparation, should also use visuals and activities that involve the learner directly in the class session.

Methods of involvement not only enhance learning, they also encourage *fellowship*. For example, I can teach the content of John 15 with a lecture, or I can divide my class into small groups to answer questions from the passage. After discussing the importance of abiding in Christ, I might ask class members to share with their group the fruit of the Spirit they presently need most. The class could conclude with members praying for one another. Both of these instructional methods teach the message of John 15, but the second method also forces students to become better acquainted. The members of a class using involvement methods will get to know one another far better than those in a class using nonparticipatory methods.

Whether in a children's, youth, or adult class, methods which utilize involvement enhance learning and encourage relationships. Better learning and better relationships result in a better quality Sunday School. A quality educational ministry produces enthusiasm and is attractive to people.

A Warm Learning Environment

Why do people install carpeting over the floors in their homes? Why do they hang curtains in their windows, or place pictures on their walls? Obviously, because these furnishings soften a home; they give it a warmer feeling. Why is it then that some churches are content with bare walls, cement or tile floors, and cold metal chairs for their Bible classes? Church facilities that communicate warmth are more conducive for learning and attracting people.

Major facility renovations are costly, but smaller outlays of dollars, wisely spent, can make a great investment in learning. For some churches this may simply mean fresh paint in the classrooms, improved lighting, or curtains for the windows. Quality floor coverings warm a room, but more importantly they help reduce sound problems. Even the noise of metal chairs is minimized with carpeting. Tables, tackboards, overhead projectors, and other equipment can transform a sterile room into an attractive learning environment.

There are many books that describe how to design good

learning environments for specific age groups—that's not my purpose here. I simply want to reinforce the fact that a warm learning environment has a direct relationship to people's receptivity and participation. The friendlier the atmosphere of a classroom (and that includes both the physical and the relational), the more likely it is that people will return.

Room for Growth

A warm learning environment has another characteristic; it says "Welcome!"—by providing room for additional people to participate. While this may seem obvious to some, I'm amazed at how many church leaders do not really practice this principle. They may say they want to grow, but their lip service is rarely transformed into behaviors that welcome newcomers. For example, they may recognize that the parking lot is full (and even see people drive off), but they resist personal requests to park across the street.

Many churches exceed 90 percent capacity of their facilities, yet find people resistant to double sessions or facility expansion. Comments such as, "We like our class the way it is," or "But we all want to worship at the same hour," are indirect ways of saying, "We're not willing to make space for new people."

An empty pew in the front of the sanctuary does not mean there is still room for growth. An architect's stated seating capacity (16½ inches per person) does not realistically determine how many people a church can accommodate. To get an accurate picture for the sanctuary, simply have a group of people sit comfortably in the pews, and then multiply their number by the number of pews. In a classroom, take the total square footage (minus clutter, pianos, cabinets, etc.) and divide it by the space requirements needed for the learners. (Early Childhood [2–kindergarten]—30–35 square feet per pupil; children [Grades 1–6]—25–30 square feet per pupil; youth [Grades 7–12]—20–25 square feet per pupil; adults [college age and up]—10–20 square feet per pupil.)

Churches that have classes with dynamic teachers and rooms that are warm and friendly will attract many people. But even with the best teacher and the nicest classroom, we discourage attendance and contribute to apathy if there is not enough space for people. Room for growth is essential to a healthy learning environment.

Sufficient Financial Resources

Most churches struggle with finances. It's a rare church (or perhaps one that hasn't planned well) that has a surplus year after year in its general fund. A large budget does not automatically produce a better program, but sufficient funding is essential for effective ministry. A teacher that is supplied with good materials communicates more effectively than a comparable teacher without materials.

Classrooms with carpeting, comfortable seating, and attractive bulletin boards enhance the learning atmosphere. Money spent on teacher-training improves the quality of classroom instruction. The return on these financial expenditures is a higher quality program, and the result of an exciting program is enthusiastic participants.

Since the church budget includes many "fixed items" (salaries, debt retirement, utilities, and missions), program areas too often are underbudgeted in relation to need. Those concerned with improving the quality of Christian education must lobby for expanding the financial base of the C.E. department.

While an effective and attractive Christian education program may not happen overnight, intentional steps each year will improve the long-range quality. For example, one overhead projector can be placed in the budget each year, until one is available for each adult/youth classroom. In the same way, money can be designated annually to send a few workers to a training seminar. Budgeting for a teacher recognition night can also take place gradually, with quality of program and meals increasing over time.

One issue worth special attention relates to budget surplus. Since the money a church receives above its budget is undesignated, I recommend that the congregation adopt a policy to use the annual surplus for designated projects. These dollars go further because they do not need to be divided among the fixed expenditures. Therefore, the Christian Education Committee will want to make sure that it maintains a list of suggestions for improving the teaching ministry of the church (training, facilities, equipment, etc.).

A Marketplace Mentality

There is nothing more uplifting to a church's self-image than to see new people joining the fellowship. When new people are attracted to a church, even the long-standing member begins to feel: "We must be doing things right if new people are coming." The infusion of new blood into the congregation is a quick cure for overcoming apathy. Church growth produces enthusiasm, and an enthusiastic church is the type of church which draws even more people.

Church leaders concerned with outreach need to recognize a changing phenomenon in our culture. Socialization has moved from the neighborhood to the workplace. Our neighbors are no longer those who live next door, but are now typically those with whom we work. Several factors have brought about this transition.

In 1984 27 million *married women* were *employed outside of the home.* Even among the "baby boomers" (those born between 1946 and 1964), who affirm a recommitment to family values, most mothers (even of preschoolers) are employed outside of the home. The last decade has also seen a sharp increase in the number of *single-parent families.* The woman talking with her neighbor across the fence, exchanging recipes, has largely disappeared.

Not only have relationships in neighborhoods decreased among women, but they have also decreased among children. Preschoolers attend Kindercare or the Learning Tree, and children participate in special enrichment programs. Neighborhood ball fields are empty as *teenagers join the workforce.* Nearly one half of our junior high and senior high young people have part-time jobs (compared to less than one fourth in 1950).

Relationships among men in their neighborhoods are also affected by societal changes. Increased technology, boredom and desire to get ahead often lead men to make vocational changes. Frequent transitions hinder people from building (or even desiring to build) deep relationships with neighbors.

Upward mobility has given families greater affluence and therefore, the means to spend leisure time away from their neighborhoods. Boats, campers, snowmobiles, and trips to Disney World have all taken a toll on neighborhood relationships.

While not neglecting our geographical neighbors, the church that is interested in outreach will motivate congregants to view the workplace or social club as their harvest field. A pastor who encourages his people to "invite a neighbor for the Christmas program," may see less response than the one who suggests, "Invite a friend from work." A church with a marketplace mentality, desiring to reach outside of its own walls, will reap the enthusiasm of new attenders.

Conclusion

Greenfields Church had grown steadily for twelve years, but plateaued when they hit 240 in attendance. For seven years they did not grow beyond that number.

When Pastor Bloomquist was called to the congregation, his first goal was to build a positive attitude in the church. He worked with the C.E. Committee to select relevant topics for Sunday School, and set up several teacher-training opportunities. Sensing that many people had a desire for Bible study and fellowship, he coordinated the start-up of a few home Bible studies. He encouraged program leaders to "have a party" with their workers at the end of the year. Time was taken to write notes of appreciation to those working in leadership and especially to commend those who cultivated friendships with nonbelievers.

In time, Pastor Bloomquist presented the elders with several models for moving into double services. He parked his car across the street and asked the leadership to do the same. He worked with the long-range planning committee, and subsequently the building committee, to construct an attractive multipurpose building. Most importantly, he continually tried to help the congregation believe that God could do even more through them than they could imagine.

The vision of Pastor Bloomquist helped Greenfields break through their 240 barrier. In fact, they have registered growth every year since. Two years ago the pastor moved on to a new ministry, but the church has continued to grow. The leaders have caught a positive vision of effective ministry, and together they are doing a better job than one man could have ever done.

Can a congregation overcome apathy and decline, and move toward a vibrant, enthusiastic ministry? Most certainly. Even churches hit by declining demographic shifts can have meaningful, and therefore positive, ministries. Whether we direct our efforts toward the Sunday School, club program, shelter for homeless, or crisis counseling center, effective ministry produces life and enthusiasm.

A Checklist for Building Enthusiasm

Does our church have...

☐ A Positive Self-Image

☐ A Format That Recognizes Differences

☐ A Competent Teaching Staff

☐ Relevant Topics of Study

☐ Methodologies That Encourage Involvement

☐ A Warm Learning Environment

☐ Room for Growth

☐ Sufficient Financial Resources

☐ A Marketplace Mentality

CHAPTER SEVEN

COORDINATION OF THE CHRISTIAN EDUCATION PROGRAM

I am not surprised that pastors ranked coordination of the overall program among the top ten educational problems. Perhaps they had the same types of situations arise as did the ones in these three churches.

The missions committee at Firestone Church was looking forward to next week's annual conference. The mother-daughter brunch was a new feature this year, and they were anticipating a good attendance. The speaker was already contacted, the basement was scheduled and the menu was planned.

The first time they realized they had a problem was when a couple of mothers mentioned that they could not attend because their daughters were participating in a Pioneer Girls activity that Saturday morning. Unfortunately, the club leaders didn't realize there was a Saturday activity that week, so they purchased tickets and promised to take the girls to a play. When they heard about the brunch, they decided to go ahead with their plans, because "most of our girls are from non-church families anyway." Needless to say, the conflict became a source of tension among both club workers and parents.

At First Church the boys club scheduled a day of horseback riding to reward the fellows for their achievements. Later that month the leaders heard that the children's choir director had called a special Saturday rehearsal, because the kids needed more practice for the upcoming concert. Poor coordination again became a source of tension.

At North Heights Church a conflict arose over use of overhead projectors. The three overheads owned by the church were usually sufficient for those who needed them, but recently the demand exceeded the supply. A couple of the teachers began to come early to make sure they got projectors. Some were still searching after classtime had begun. One teacher stopped preparing transparencies altogether. The lack of coordination regarding equipment became divisive.

In these three illustrations, planning was not the central issue; each of the teachers had planned well his own activity. The problem these workers experienced was one of coordination. Conflicts arose over the use of equipment, rooms, or the involvement of participants.

Poor coordination of personnel can lead to overworking some people, while overlooking others. Poor coordination of programs leads to duplication in some areas and neglect in others. Coordination is essential to staffing, program content, program scheduling, and facility usage.

An effective ministry is a well-coordinated ministry. It accomplishes the church's purposes without duplication of its resources. Four ingredients are essential for good coordination: a positive team spirit; a functional Christian education committee; a responsible decision-making process; and an annual assessment.

A Positive Team Attitude

You probably recognize by now that I believe *good attitudes* are critical to Christian education. Effective Christian education is not simply an issue of teachers, curriculum, and students. It is primarily the attitudes that we have about our teachers, and the attitudes they have about their curriculum and students. Healthy, positive attitudes produce healthy Christian education programs. Disruptive, negative attitudes result in discouraging Christian education programs.

Frequently I am asked whether one type of church board structure is superior to another. While I believe there are some advantages to a unified board, the bottom line in any system is the people in it. A quality person will serve faithfully whether he is called an elder or a deacon; a cranky, obnoxious leader is cancerous whether he is called an elder or a deacon. If I had to choose between a contentious, highly talented leader, and a positive, lesser-skilled worker, I'd take the positive person every time.

There is no greater wet blanket to ministry than leadership with the attitude, "We can't do it." But there is nothing more encouraging to ministry than a leader who affirms, "I can do everything through Him [Christ] who gives me strength" (Phil. 4:13).

The first step in bringing coordination to the overall education program, is to cultivate a positive team spirit among those serving. This task begins by helping people understand that "we is they." You've probably heard people say: "I wish *they'd* quit taking my chairs"; or "*They* never buy enough materials"; or "Why won't *they* give us a larger room?" These comments come from people who subconsciously act as though there's some kind of war going on.

A congregation cannot afford a "we versus they" mentality. It must fight this false dichotomy. We *is* the they; they *is* the we. The real enemy is Satan and his forces of wickedness. Yet we get so caught up in our individual programs that anyone who seems to disagree or hinder us is viewed as an adversary.

A "we versus they" mentality can develop between pastor and people, program leaders and trustees, C.E. workers and those involved in music ministry, or even those who attend prayer meeting and those who participate in a home Bible study. Christians will have different functions within the ministry, but they are all part of the same team. There is no "they"; there is only the "we." When conflict arises, it's not my problem or their problem, but rather our problem. As a cooperative attitude develops among the staff, conflicts diminish.

A church with a positive team spirit demonstrates flexibility when inadvertant conflicts arise. For example, because of the healthy staff relationships in the church with the overhead projector problem, a solution was worked out. One of the leaders began to bring a projector home from work on Friday evenings to use in his adult class. One teacher switched to a chalkboard, and two teachers alternated usage every other week. Furthermore, the C.E. Committee placed a request for two new projectors in the upcoming budget.

A positive team spirit is also enhanced when people in one program know what's happening in another program. The typical Sunday School teacher or youth sponsor is so involved in his own ministry that he rarely is aware of developments in the nursery or home Bible study. Program awareness is increasingly difficult the larger the church is. Nevertheless, an increased awareness of other programs helps workers feel that they're part of an overall team.

Awareness is facilitated by a *master calendar* to coordinate room reservations, equipment, etc., through one centralized office. Typically, a church secretary will handle requests and make tentative schedules (pending board approval). While many churches utilize a calendar for recording requests, too few use it to communicate back to program leaders the overall annual planning. Regular distributions of scheduled activities to workers make them aware of other activities taking place. The two-way calendar is an indispensable tool for coordination and communication.

Regular communication of events is also facilitated through positive articles in a *church newsletter*. Program leaders can take a moment at staff meetings to bring updates of what's happening in other programs. Christian education workers that enjoy their own ministries, and who appreciate the service of team members, are more responsive to coordination efforts.

A Functional C.E. Committee
The best guarantee for a balanced, coordinated education program is the supervisory work of a Christian Education Committee. Churches able to afford a minister of Christian education benefit greatly from this professional oversight. Nevertheless, all size churches derive profit from a good committee that meets periodically to establish policy, coordinate programs, and assist in personnel matters.

First, the *organization* of a Christian Education Committee can, by its very composition, help coordinate an overall program. A good organizational form for coordinating the educational ministry is to have program directors comprise the committee. For example, a C.E. Committee may consist of:

- The Sunday School superintendent
- The children's church coordinator
- The director of the club program
- A youth sponsor
- The personnel coordinator
- The pastor (or representative from the church board).

Larger congregations have seen the value of utilizing age-group coordinators. With this arrangement the Christian Education Committee will look like this:

- Early childhood coordinator
- Children's coordinator
- Youth coordinator
- Adult coordinator
- Personnel coordinator
- Representative from the pastoral staff.

Coordination of the educational program with the overall church ministry is best accomplished through a unified board system (i.e., a deacon or elder serving on each subcommittee) or through a church council.

Second, the Christian Education Committee coordinates its ministry through the *adoption of programs*. For example, two years ago Bethany Church began a club program for its boys. The new program was so exciting that some parents wanted to change the existing girl's program to the same publisher as the boy's work. In a church where leaders are allowed to do their own thing, a real squabble over the girl's program could have developed. But at Bethany Church, the Christian Education Committee received the request, reviewed the program, and shared with the parents a good rationale for keeping the existing girl's program.

The experience of Sunnyside Church provides a similar example. For over two decades Sunnyside had conducted a two-week Vacation Bible School (VBS) each August, but over the past few years it had become nearly impossible to find enough workers. For many, vacation time was a conflict; others felt they lost momentum in the ten-day school.

A request came from the Vacation Bible School coordinator and the children's coordinator to try a one-week Bible school. Some on the committee felt that the recommendation was a move away from Bible teaching. Others saw a real potential for holding the children's interest, and for staff recruitment. After much discussion the committee agreed to try a five-day VBS, with a closing carnival on Friday evening. The new format was so well received by both the community and teaching staff that they have maintained the one-week format for the last few years.

The change to a one-week school would have caused dissension if the decision was made only by the Christian education director or the VBS coordinator. But because of the unanimous recommendation of the Christian Education Committee, the congregation was ready to move in a new direction.

Whether the issue is beginning a children's church, switching VBS to evenings, or the beginning of a Bible study at a retirement village, the Christian Education Committee is the place where pros and cons are evaluated, and programs are coordinated. Group decisions are safer than unilateral decisions. Remember, "Many advisers make victory sure" (Prov. 11:14).

Third, the Christian Education Committee coordinates ministry through *approval of curriculum*. In the Old Testament we read that there was no king in Israel, and all the people did what was right in their own eyes (Judges 17:6). Unfortunately, many educational programs run the same way. Adult teachers do their own thing. Children's workers purchase and use whatever is appealing. And who knows what goes on in some home Bible studies? However, a church that takes seriously its Christian education responsibility will make sure that its people have a balanced and thorough understanding of the Scriptures.

For this reason many churches follow the scope and sequence of one publishing house to assure coordination in the Sunday School. These materials will typically highlight major Bible concepts in the preschool years; cycle through the Scriptures again in story and history form in the childhood years; give a balance of Old Testament, New Testament, and contemporary issues in the youth years; and offer expository and topical studies for adults.

Coordination of curriculum across educational programs is possible once the curriculum is determined for the most highly attended ministry. Since Sunday School is the program with the largest attendance, curriculum for other programs can be built around themes in the Sunday School. Duplication, or neglect, of Scripture is eliminated through requiring C.E. Committee approval for all teaching materials.

At Paradise Cathedral, the youth pastor developed a six-year curriculum for the Sunday School. Not satisfied with one particular publisher for the entire youth division, he selected a balanced diet of subjects for his teens. The comprehensive plan was approved by the Christian Education Committee, yet he selected the best publisher for each specific topic. By charting out the Sunday School program of study, he was able to plan his Wednesday evening gatherings and retreat themes around topics not currently covered in Sunday School.

The average teacher does not have the skills or time to objectively evaluate curriculum. The C.E. Committee, with responsibility for the overall program, is better able to study alternatives and make sound decisions (a form for evaluating curriculum is included at the end of this chapter).

Fourth, the Christian Education Committee encourages coordination by *appointing educational workers.* While names of prospective workers are cleared through a personnel committee, and the recruitment of teachers is made by the program leaders, actual appointments to service are assigned by the Christian Education Committee. Teachers that are poorly recruited rarely feel a part of the big picture. But when the Christian Education Committee welcomes a teacher to the educational faculty, and commissions him for service, the worker feels a part of a team.

The Christian Education Committee's effectiveness in coordination is directly related to its effectiveness in conducting business. *Profitable meetings* are essential for program management. Committees function best when limited to four to nine members. A committee comprised of coordinators (who actually supervise their areas of ministry) could meet as few as four to six times per year. Other committees would profit from monthly meetings.

A *planned agenda* is a must for all meetings. Committee members should know ahead of time whether program updates are expected and be informed of issues scheduled for general discussion. *Handouts* distributed prior to the actual meeting allow time for study by committee members. The *length* of time for meetings is best kept between seventy-five to ninety minutes. A meeting deadline will expedite business and avoid the free rolling discussions that distract from the committee's charge.

A Responsible Decision-Making Process

The pastor of Bloomfield Church made a classic blunder. Concerned with their rapid growth, he worked with the church council to develop a plan for double services. The elders understood that they should *consider several solutions before selecting the best solution.* However, when the first announcement was made to the congregation, flack from a few key people awakened them to the realization that they had failed to *involve significant people* in the overall process.

The double-session arrangement had implications for both worship and the Sunday School. And while the C.E. leadership was in agreement with the plan, individual Christian education workers were never asked their opinions. The first time Mrs. Townsend knew that her class was switched from 9:45 to 11:00 was when she read it in the church newsletter.

One year later the leadership at Bloomfield Church had to make another decision. This time they involved many people in the process, and subsequently *gave early communication* of the decision. The church council was concerned with developing a comprehensive shepherding program. Too many visitors and infrequent attenders were slipping through the cracks. So they approached the Christian Education Committee with the possibility of using the adult Sunday School for the shepherding program. The C.E. leadership surveyed the adults and then made a recommendation to switch from an elective system to a stage-graded format.

The council targeted the following fall to begin the program, but used the intervening months to communicate the reasons for the change. They wanted enough time to present the benefits of the stage-graded structure and to answer objections honestly. They used the church newsletter for congregationwide communication, but also interacted individually with people, sharing their enthusiasm for this new approach to caring. The early communication by the leadership, and the enthusiasm of the teachers once the program began, produced a climate of acceptance.

A responsible decision-making process also *anticipates the consequences of decisions.* In the case of Bloomfield Church, they offered one elective class for those who preferred the old system, and they even scheduled several intergenerational activities. Now after three years they have only the fellowship-grouped classes, and each of the age groups is thriving. Broad involvement, the best solution, and early communication helped them change a twenty-year tradition into a well-received ministry.

A Periodic Assessment

Home, comfort, familiarity—change, disruption, the unknown. Which set of words makes you feel better? Most people are content with the familiar and established; churches are no exception. It is easier to perpetuate programs that are familiar and comfortable than to evaluate whether they are the best possible ministries for the present situation. A periodic assessment can help people critically evaluate the meaningfulness of a program. Furthermore, the assessment can reveal whether the ministry mix is balanced and in harmony with biblical purposes.

Clark Summit Church developed its mission statement from Colossians 1:28: "that we may present all people mature in Christ." They sought to accomplish this endeavor by being a community for worship, a classroom for education, a family for fellowship, and a task force for evangelism. Now it's easy to add a mission statement to a constitution, but the question remains: How are we measuring up to our purposes? Clark Summit decided to assess its program.

One Thursday evening the church board convened for an evaluation session. The moderator drew a grid on the blackboard. He listed their four purposes horizontally, and asked the group to delineate their programs vertically. As a program was mentioned, he asked the council to identify whether it was in the category of worship (adoration of God), education (Christian learning), fellowship (caring and sharing), evangelism (witness, missions, and social concerns), or a combination of those. Their chart looked like Figure 7-1 on page 123.

The chart constructed by the church board yielded a bird's-eye view of the church's overall ministry. Initially the leadership was concerned that they provide more fellowship for the congregation, but when the moderator finished placing the last √, they saw two other areas with greater need.

The most glaring neglect was evangelism. Except for periodic invitations by the pastor in the morning service, or an occasional conversion in the children's Sunday School or VBS, the church was doing little corporate evangelism. The board recognized that the church gathered for worship, education, and fellowship and scattered for evangelism. They felt that as a congregation more intentionality was needed in witness and social concern. Their second observation noted the limited opportunities for worship. Corporate adoration of God only took place in the Sunday services, and perhaps during choir rehearsals.

As a result of the self-study, home Bible study leaders were encouraged to include singing of choruses and expressing praise as part of their weekly meetings. The outreach committee made contacts with the Red Cross, and the church became a center for regular blood donation drives. The committee also scheduled a community recreation night once a week in the gymnasium to build bridges with neighbors. In addition, the evangelism committee laid plans for beginning an Evangelism Explosion program. Clark Summit's self-study helped them assess their program mix and identify areas for program development. The study was also beneficial to the budgeting process, for it revealed areas that needed additional support for effectiveness.

A periodic assessment was also profitable to Berean Church. Their study identified programs by age groups. As a result of their evaluation they realized they needed to do more for their children. Their age-group program comparison looked like Figure 7-2 on page 124.

As a result of the study, Berean began an after-school club program for third through sixth grades. A year later the church formed a children's choir, which met during the second part of the morning worship service. As in the case of Clark Summit Church, Berean Church was able to better coordinate its overall ministry because the leaders assessed the program mix in light of their church's mission and purpose.

Conclusion

The average church member probably spends more time in front of his television than in private devotions and church activities combined. Unfortunately, many even watch more hours of programming in one evening than their total participation in church programming during an entire week. The influence of secular values hits our people outside the home as well as within. The adversary's public relations techniques are slick, but we are not ignorant of his schemes.

Therefore, it is imperative that churches plan and provide a quality Christian education program for their people. Pastors and program leaders must resist mediocrity; every sermon and every teaching session must be a vital component which maximizes spiritual growth.

A quality ministry with a balanced program does not take place by accident. Good coordination of the entire educational ministry requires healthy teacher attitudes, good organization, wise decisions, and regular evaluation. A well-orchestrated program encourages participation and fosters Christian maturity.

Self-Study of Clark Summit Church

PROGRAMS	WORSHIP	EDUCATION	FELLOWSHIP	EVANGELISM
A.M. Service	✓	✓		✓
P.M. Service	✓	✓	✓	
P.M. Orchestra	✓			
Children's S.S.		✓	✓	✓
Adult S.S.		✓	✓	
Children's Church	✓	✓		
Kid's Choir	✓	✓	✓	
Adult Choir	✓		✓	
Library		✓		
Boys Club		✓	✓	
Girls Club		✓	✓	
Youth Alive		✓	✓	
Prayer Meeting	✓	✓		
Home Bible Studies		✓	✓	
Men's Group		✓	✓	
Women's Bible Studies		✓	✓	
Nursery			✓	
Missions Conference		✓		✓
Vacation Bible School		✓		✓
Youth Activities			✓	
Family Camp		✓	✓	
Weekday Preschool		✓	✓	

Figure 7-1.

Age-Group Program Mix

PROGRAMS	PRESCHOOLERS	CHILDREN	YOUTH	ADULTS
A.M. Worship	✓	✓	✓	✓
P.M. Worship	✓	✓	✓	✓
Choir				✓
Sunday School	✓	✓	✓	✓
Prayer Meeting			✓	✓
Women Alive	✓			✓
Mother's Day Out	✓			✓
Home Bible Studies				✓
Cottage Prayer Meetings				✓
Counseling Service				✓
Library	✓	✓	✓	✓
VBS		✓	✓	
Gathering			✓	
The Weekender			✓	
Retreats			✓	✓
Church Picnic	✓	✓	✓	✓

Figure 7-2.

A Checklist for Coordination

Does our church have . . .

☐ A Positive Team Spirit

☐ A Functional Christian Education Committee

☐ A Responsible Decision-Making Process

☐ An Annual Assessment

Criteria for Evaluating Curriculum

When a Christian education committee decides to evaluate its Sunday School curriculum, what kinds of issues should be considered? Use the following questions to examine the content, design, teaching methods, and appearance of your curriculum materials. Place an X in the rating box you feel is most appropriate. There is room provided to add any points of special interest that you would like to evaluate your curriculum against.

I. Content: What Does It Say?

	Not applicable	None	Poor	Average	Good	Excellent
A. Bible Orientation						
1. Are the Scriptures treated as the fully inspired Word of God?	☐	☐	☐	☐	☐	☐
2. Are biblical passages interpreted accurately and meaningfully?	☐	☐	☐	☐	☐	☐
3. Are accurate translations used?	☐	☐	☐	☐	☐	☐
4. Other _____	☐	☐	☐	☐	☐	☐
B. Christian Values						
1. Is a distinctly Christian value system taught?	☐	☐	☐	☐	☐	☐
2. Are issues raised which cause students to examine their own values?	☐	☐	☐	☐	☐	☐
3. Are students helped to choose Christian values?	☐	☐	☐	☐	☐	☐
4. Other _____	☐	☐	☐	☐	☐	☐
C. Life Issues						
1. Are critical life issues raised?	☐	☐	☐	☐	☐	☐
2. Are current life problems realistically presented?	☐	☐	☐	☐	☐	☐

3. Are simplistic, pat answers avoided? ☐ ☐ ☐ ☐ ☐ ☐
4. Other _____ ☐ ☐ ☐ ☐ ☐ ☐

D. Age-Group Related
1. Is the content appropriate for its intended age group? ☐ ☐ ☐ ☐ ☐ ☐
2. Are appropriate age-level Bible study methods used? ☐ ☐ ☐ ☐ ☐ ☐
3. Are contemporary interests of the age group mentioned? ☐ ☐ ☐ ☐ ☐ ☐
4. Other _____ ☐ ☐ ☐ ☐ ☐ ☐

II. Educational Philosophy: How Does It Teach?
A. Life Orientation
1. Are students challenged to make life responses, rather than just to understand facts? ☐ ☐ ☐ ☐ ☐ ☐
2. Does curriculum show students how to apply biblical principles? ☐ ☐ ☐ ☐ ☐ ☐
3. Is application stressed as much as interpretation? ☐ ☐ ☐ ☐ ☐ ☐
4. Other _____ ☐ ☐ ☐ ☐ ☐ ☐

B. Response Orientation
1. Are students led to respond to biblical teaching? ☐ ☐ ☐ ☐ ☐ ☐
2. Are students allowed to respond as individuals, each as creatively special? ☐ ☐ ☐ ☐ ☐ ☐
3. Do responses affect various areas of students' lives? ☐ ☐ ☐ ☐ ☐ ☐
4. Other _____ ☐ ☐ ☐ ☐ ☐ ☐

C. Home and Family Orientation

127

1. Is the home and family properly emphasized? ☐ ☐ ☐ ☐ ☐ ☐
2. Are there attempts made to strengthen the home, its value, and importance? ☐ ☐ ☐ ☐ ☐ ☐
3. Are contemporary home and family situations adequately considered? ☐ ☐ ☐ ☐ ☐ ☐
4. Other _____ ☐ ☐ ☐ ☐ ☐ ☐

III. Teaching Methods: How Does It Help the Teacher?

A. Creative Techniques
1. Are students required to actively participate in the lessons? ☐ ☐ ☐ ☐ ☐ ☐
2. Is the teacher encouraged to use a variety of teaching methods? ☐ ☐ ☐ ☐ ☐ ☐
3. Other _____ ☐ ☐ ☐ ☐ ☐ ☐

B. Teaching Aids
1. Are a variety of teaching aids provided? ☐ ☐ ☐ ☐ ☐ ☐
2. Are the teaching aids easily adapted to a variety of situations? ☐ ☐ ☐ ☐ ☐ ☐
3. Is the teacher guided in their proper use? ☐ ☐ ☐ ☐ ☐ ☐
4. Do the books containing student handwork present projects within students' capabilities? ☐ ☐ ☐ ☐ ☐ ☐
5. Other _____ ☐ ☐ ☐ ☐ ☐ ☐

C. Study Aids

1. Is the teacher encouraged to do additional study for each lesson? ☐ ☐ ☐ ☐ ☐ ☐

2. Are resource suggestions made for additional study pertaining to the lesson topic? ☐ ☐ ☐ ☐ ☐ ☐

3. Are suggestions made for additional study for teaching methods? ☐ ☐ ☐ ☐ ☐ ☐

4. Other _____ ☐ ☐ ☐ ☐ ☐ ☐

D. Flexibility
1. Is the curriculum adaptable to a variety of situations? ☐ ☐ ☐ ☐ ☐ ☐

2. Are various levels of ability for both students and teacher considered? ☐ ☐ ☐ ☐ ☐ ☐

3. Other _____ ☐ ☐ ☐ ☐ ☐ ☐

IV. Appearance: How Does it Look

A. Does the layout attract the student to deeper involvement? ☐ ☐ ☐ ☐ ☐ ☐

B. Is the use of color attractive to students? ☐ ☐ ☐ ☐ ☐ ☐

C. Are pictures and artwork used advantageously? ☐ ☐ ☐ ☐ ☐ ☐

D. Will the material withstand heavy use? ☐ ☐ ☐ ☐ ☐ ☐

E. Other _____ ☐ ☐ ☐ ☐ ☐ ☐

CHAPTER EIGHT

LACK OF USE OF THE CHURCH LIBRARY

Each Thursday morning Nancy Hardwick, Kathy Crenshaw, and Eva Swanson meet together at the church. Kathy brings goodies from the bake shop, and Eva brings a large thermos of coffee. Sometimes they spend only a couple of hours together; other times they meet all day. These women are quite different, yet they have a common cause that unites them. Their love for good reading, and their desire to make growth resources available to others, keeps them meeting week after week to process books and promote their church library. With this type of leadership it's not surprising that the library at Centerton Church is used regularly.

Church libraries come in different sizes and are found in various campus locations. Some libraries are little more than a modest collection of books kept in a closet or displayed on a table. Other libraries boast of thousands of titles, each kept on display in a spacious media center. Some churches report that their libraries are used regularly, while many churches, regardless of size, report little or no use of their church libraries. What makes the difference?

If pastor or people view their library as an obsolete collection of irrelevant books, then no one should get upset if the library is not used. But if they believe that the library is an excellent tool of Christian education, that it can expand teaching hours beyond the classroom, and that it can give personal instruction to people with a variety of needs, then they should take every step necessary to make it successful.

Libraries that are well used display several common characteristics. Successful church libraries have: key leaders, knowledgeable personnel, a visible location, convenient hours, a diversified collection, purchasing options, regular promotion, and adequate finances.

Key Leaders

Recently I talked with a pastor whose church library circulates 3,000 books each month. Not only does the library service the church membership, but the pastor believes the library is their greatest contact with the community. When I asked him what made their library successful, he immediately gave me the name of one woman who, for twenty years, has made the library her personal ministry. "She is so aware of new children's books," he related, "that I play a game with her. Whenever I read a review on a new children's book, I ask her if she has it yet. Invariably she reports, 'It's already been purchased!' "

Locate any effective library, and behind the scenes you'll find effective leadership administering it. Perhaps only one person heads the project, or like the church in Centerton, a team of people may hold the common vision. If the pastor or members are interested in good literature, but the church cannot find someone to organize the library, then that need will go unmet. A church interested in developing a ministry through Christian books or tapes must identify a person who carries a burden for that work. If no one in the congregation desires to serve in the library, a viable media ministry is unlikely.

While a sense of ownership is important for a good librarian, expertise in library science is not. In fact, the woman who manages the library in my friend's church knew very little about libraries when she began. She acquired her knowledge through local seminars and even traveled to some regional workshops to pick up additional insights. It was her deep commitment to see Christian literature in the hands of God's people that led her to challenge the leadership and congregation to build and use a church library.

Knowledgeable Personnel
Although a few leaders are essential to develop a good library, the day-to-day ministry of the library requires additional personnel. A librarian, or library committee, gives special attention to the selection, processing, and promotion of media. Other volunteers can assist people who come to use the library.

We've all appreciated the grocery clerk who can tell us, "The taco seasoning is in aisle fifteen." Similarly, knowledgeable personnel in the library can help people locate materials which may interest them. Workers are not present just to make sure books are checked out properly. Primarily they are sales persons who know their products well and try to encourage customers to try them: "I'm sorry, Dobson's book is checked out, but have you seen Jay Kesler's latest book on parenting?"

Key leaders, supported by knowledgeable personnel, will not only build a good library, but a good reputation for it as well. In turn, a library with a good reputation will build an ever-widening circle of satisfied users.

A Visible Location
When my wife and I looked for a new home our realtor told us that there are three critical factors regarding housing: "location, location, and location." I think he made his point—location is important.

A library can have competent leadership and friendly personnel, but if it's housed in an obscure location where people rarely travel, it's dead. Very few people will come early to church or stick around afterwards to look for the library.

By way of contrast, the library placed right in the middle of the church's hottest traffic pattern will experience high consumer usage. One church, for example, moved their library into a former classroom off the main sidewalk that connected the parking lot to the sanctuary. In another church the staff offices were relocated to allow the library to have their former space adjacent to the coatroom and sanctuary. The new location helped the church immensely with utilizing the library.

If it is not possible to improve the location of your library, try doing what Village Church did. Their pastor asked a carpenter to build a tiered, portable display rack. Books, records, and even cassette tapes are checked out, and later returned through a slot in the side of the unit. The 5' x 5' rack attractively fits into the decor of the foyer, and the library staff regularly rotates the display inventory.

What makes a successful library? Among other variables, remember the importance of location, location, location.

Convenient Hours

When are people regularly on your church grounds—Sunday mornings? Wednesday evenings? Friday mornings? Effective libraries are open whenever groups of people are using the church facilities. Do you have a mothers' day out? Have the library open. Does the Red Cross periodically use your facilities as a collection site? Have the library open. Whenever a significant event is taking place, keep the library open before, during, and after the activities.

By way of reminder let me emphasize the importance of all factors working together to maximize library usage. A library open forty hours a week, but housed in the basement of the youth building will only find an occasional wayfarer. But a library that already has good leadership, helpful workers, and a good location will also profit from opening fifteen or thirty minutes before and after a regular service.

A number of churches make their library available during the Sunday School hour. Some even rotate small groups of children into the library to hear a story or check out a book or record. Young people have been sent to libraries to do a brief research project and then report back to their classes.

The library is also a good vehicle for community outreach. In one church for example, the preschool director sets a coffee pot next to the library as a place for parents to share in friendly conversation. Many of the moms check out books and tapes for their children, but also novels or books on marriage and parenting. Whenever a program brings people to the church campus is a good time for an open library.

Many churches short of Christian education space use their library as a Sunday School room. Unfortunately this doubling-up of space takes a disastrous toll on library utilization. Not only does the arrangement prohibit the use of the library during the class hour, but it typically discourages use before and after Sunday School. Rarely will people visit a library before Sunday School if chairs are stacked in the room, set up for class. Neither do classes finish early enough to permit browsing between Sunday School and the worship hour. A library with its own space can use optimal time periods to promote its Christian growth materials.

A Diversified Collection

Good church libraries display variety in their resources. Since materials are costly and budgets limited, churches will wisely stock items that have a high consumption rate. For example, while Bible commentaries are important and every church should have some, they are not frequently borrowed items. Multiple sets of reference works are not the best use of funds.

Some churches interested in beginning a library have put out the welcome mat for donated books. Unfortunately, many donated books are dated and unattractive, and therefore of little interest to people. This is exemplified by a 1940s book about West Point that I discovered in one church library. Needless to say there was not a single signature on the loan card. What a waste of processing time and shelf space.

Libraries can profit by receiving donated books, but it is wise to publicize a policy that openly states: "All donations are welcomed, however duplicate items or books with limited appeal will be passed on to interested parties."

Since people's taste and preference differ, diversity will characterize the good library. Shelves should display reference materials as well as popular books. The library should promote biographies with appeal to the old and storybooks of interest to the young. Since young women typically are its greatest consumers, a good library will take that age group into special consideration, both for their own tastes and for items they would select for their children.

Good libraries will keep in mind that many adults are non-readers (some statistics assert that one out of every four men is a nonreader, this aside from the number of poor readers). It is not surprising, therefore, that many churches notice a substantial increase in the popularity of their library when they begin a *cassette tape* ministry. People traveling in their cars, or working around the house, can double the use of their time with cassettes.

One church began stocking contemporary Christian music *recordings,* including records, tapes, and Compact Discs. Soon they found their teens not only checking out the music, but also other library materials. *Audio storybooks* are interesting to young children, and *videocassettes* are growing in popularity with all ages.

To assure diversity and balance in the library, it is helpful to have more than one person responsible for selecting resources. Since suggestions always outnumber acquisitions, a selection committee can prioritize them in relation to balance and anticipated consumer use. The pastor, library committee members, and congregants known as good readers, are good sources for recommendations.

A library that appeals to old and young, to readers and nonreaders, and to all the people who make up our diverse congregations, will experience frequent use.

Purchasing Options

Just as some people prefer to listen to a cassette tape rather than read a book, similarly some people prefer to purchase a book rather than to borrow one. For example, I like to underline and make marginal notes in the books I read. When I go back to a book for a specific quote or idea, I usually can locate the place by my markings. Therefore, the majority of books that I read are ones that I own. Some folks like to read a book; then give it away. Some are building home libraries. Some purchase a book to give to a friend on a special occasion. The option to purchase books through a church library increases its usefulness.

If railroads had viewed themselves as being in the transportation business (instead of the train business), then today the railroads might own the airlines. A library that views its ministry as loaning books, will miss out on potential clients. But the library that sees its role as distributing Christian growth materials by loan or purchase will serve a broader clientele. This was the experience of Brentwood Church when they placed in their library a display rack with popular topics for purchase similar to those seen in commercial stores. They stocked the rack with popular titles that were for sale. This feature of their library cost them nothing. They received the rack and books on consignment from a local distributor.

While the church library should not become a bookstore, it is possible to make available for purchase a selective group of books for people who prefer to buy.

Regular Promotion

The old saying, "Out of sight, out of mind," is applicable to church libraries. Familiarity and routine will lead people past even the most visible library. In order to keep this important ministry fresh in parishioners' minds, some churches have developed a marketing strategy for visibility. While no amount of hype will make a poor library successful, periodic promotion will help the good library reach out even more.

Some churches use a "library corner" in a bulletin to promote new acquisitions in the library. Other churches with nursery schools use their newsletters to publicize the availability of parenting materials. Some librarians have asked adult Sunday School teachers to help select, and promote to their classes, books that parallel the current subject. Some pastors have made it their practice to quote an author or cite an illustration, purposely indicating that the book is available in the church library.

During library month the pastor in one church interviewed a suspicious-looking character wearing a hat and trenchcoat who was identified as "the bookie man." When the pastor asked him why he was called the bookie man, dozens of books fell from the loaded trench coat. As the books were picked up, interchange between the men promoted the titles, as well as the library in general. The jesting of that pastor and associate pastor (the bookie man) added some light-hearted moments to their evening service, but more importantly, it let the people know that the staff was very positive about the church library.

Whether a congregation uses a bookmark inserted in the bulletin, a quotation from the pulpit, or a summer reading contest, regular promotion helps maximize the usage of a good library.

Adequate Finances

Another expression we hear frequently is: "You get what you pay for." A church cannot budget only $50 or $100 for its library, then expect people to flock in. Any congregation serious about providing library resources for growth will need several hundred dollars annually in its Christian education budget.

Library committees (or the C.E. Committee) should decide whether they prefer to purchase paperbacks or hardbacks. While hardcovers are more durable, limited budgets versus thousands of titles make paperbacks very attractive.

Reminding people of the library's silent but powerful ministry may lead to direct gifts to the library. Some church libraries have received memorial gifts. Others have an annual Library Sunday. Books on consignment from a local Christian supplier are displayed on tables in the narthex. Members are encouraged to purchase a title, read it, and then donate it to the library. Exchanging copies of non-copyrighted cassette messages is a way two churches increased their resources. There are many creative ways for building the holdings of a good library.

The wisest expenditure of money is the purchasing of materials with the highest possible circulation. Since so many titles are on the market, it is beneficial to buy books with good reviews, or that come highly recommended. The poorest expenditure of money is to buy a book, cassette, record, or video that few people will check out. Purchasing items on sale, and selecting highly recommended titles and authors, will enhance the usage of the good church library.

Conclusion

The Apostle Paul revealed his strategy of evangelism when he explained that to the Jews he became a Jew, and to the Gentiles he became a Gentile, that by all means he may lead some to Christ (1 Cor. 9:19-22). Likewise, leaders concerned with nurturing Christians will use all available means to help believers in their Christian walk.

Participation in periodic worship and Bible study is profitable, but let's not overlook a means of nurture which can enhance learning daily. The effective church library makes growth materials available to everyone at his own learning level and related to his own interests.

While many churches are experiencing a lack of interest in their church libraries, other congregations have a dynamic library ministry. We live in an age that has a plethora of good educational material. Colorful children's stories, quick-moving adventures, penetrating biographies, reputable commentaries, contemporary music, practical cassettes, and family videos are just the tip of the iceberg. The well-run, well-stocked church library is not an appendix of Christian education. Rather, the effective library is a vital tool for both education and evangelism.

A Checklist for Church Libraries

Does our church have . . .

☐ Key Leaders

☐ Knowledgeable Personnel

☐ A Visible Location

☐ Convenient Hours

☐ A Diversified Collection

☐ Purchasing Options

☐ Regular Promotion

☐ Adequate Finances

JOB DESCRIPTION

Library Committee Member

DEFINITION

A library committee member is one of four persons who shares the responsibility of organizing and directing the church library.

RELATIONSHIPS

1. Appointed by the Christian Education Committee in September for a two-year term of service.
2. Responsible to the Christian Education Committee.
3. Under the supervision of the Librarian (selected by the Library Committee from one of its four members).

SPECIFIC RESPONSIBILITIES

1. Each year select a Librarian to chair the Committee.
2. Implement the library policies set by the Christian Education Committee.
3. Alert departments to new library acquisitions, demonstrating the same.
4. Make recommendations to the Christian Education Committee regarding policies and library procedures.
5. Be alert to the needs of the church and the various age divisions.
6. Assume responsibility for shelving and processing acceptable books.
7. Assume responsibility for the checking out and returning of materials, and the issuing of overdue notices.

8. Maintain definite library hours to complement regular program hours.
9. Maintain financial records. Write proposed budget and submit it to the Christian Education Committee.
10. Attend Christian education conferences with other members of the educational faculty.
11. Assume responsibility for promotion of the library.
12. Be aware of the availability of additional resource materials.

QUALIFICATIONS

1. A Christian with a Christ-honoring lifestyle.
2. A member of the church.
3. Experience in or familiarity with library operations.
4. An interest and desire to establish and promote the church library.
5. One who supports the total church program of worship, teaching, fellowship, evangelism, and stewardship.

Guidelines for Book Selection

1. Is the book true to biblical ideals and doctrines? Only books that contribute to the goals of the church belong in the church library.

2. Is the price of the book in balance with the library budget, or would its purchase prohibit the purchase of other needed books?

3. Is the subject matter fairly discussed or is the author decidedly biased?

4. Is the material covered factual, accurate, reliable, authoritative, and up-to-date?

5. Will the book appeal to the age or interest group for whom it is written?

6. Is the style of the book attractive? Some Christian books fall short of meeting high standards of form and style. Make sure the books chosen are up-to-date in content and format.

7. Is the physical makeup of the book satisfactory? Will the paper and binding hold up well under hard use? Is the print clear and easy to read? Many books are available only in paperback. Higher quality paper and better binding assure a longer life.

8. Do the illustrations complement the text and give it increased instructional value? Is the subject matter arranged logically? Is it clearly outlined and indexed so that a reader can find certain information without reading the entire book? Readers tend to choose the more appropriately and attractively illustrated book. Christian books are notorious for out-of-date pictures.

9. Have the author and publisher established good reputations for books in the field?

10. Has the volume been included in recent book lists, or has it been reviewed in contemporary periodicals?

From Elmer L. Towns and Cyril J. Barber. Successful Church Libraries. *(Grand Rapids, Mich.: Baker Book House, 1971), pp. 37–39. Used by permission.*

CHAPTER NINE

RESISTANCE TO CHANGE

L et me introduce you to four individuals who typify many people in our churches.

Gloria is a Sunday School teacher in the three-year-old department. She loves the children, enjoys her teaching ministry and has continued in that department for over three years. Last fall, however, her positive attitude quickly changed. Her irritability and defensiveness coincided with the Christian Education Committee's decision to switch curriculum. Gloria would no longer be allowed to use her favorite materials. While Gloria continued teaching in the department, she made it clear that she didn't like the change.

Though Jeff had been teaching fourth-grade boys for over a year, the new superintendent only recently became aware of trouble in his class. Whether his problem was discomfort with the teacher's manual, or that he simply did not prepare properly, Jeff repeatedly spent classtime reviewing the books of the Bible or playing Bible baseball. At department training meetings he agreed to follow the quarterly, but after a few weeks he would again drift into doing his own thing. Jeff simply wanted to do what he was comfortable doing; he resisted change.

Nancy worked in the nursery for almost a decade and believed that all Christians should serve willingly. But when the nursery committee began to talk about employing a paid nursery attendant to work with the volunteers, she was furious. The chairman of the committee met with Nancy to explain that the worker's presence during all the services would ease the rotation schedule, but more importantly, familiarity with the "resident grandma" would reduce some anxiety within the children. Nancy wasn't convinced. In fact, she laid down the ultimatum that she would resign if someone were hired. Six weeks later, the day the new attendant arrived, was the last day Nancy served in the church.

Fred was a charter member of his church, but eventually he didn't like how fast it was growing. When the deacons announced that the church would begin double sessions, and he learned that his Sunday School class was switched to 11:00 A.M., he started visiting other churches. Though he eventually came back, he never did return to his Bible class. Going to church at 9:30 A.M. and Sunday School afterwards was a change he could not handle.

These illustrations are not isolated incidents. Each of us could give dozens of examples in which people have demonstrated a resistance to change. Sometimes the resistance is mild. Other times it comes in the form of blackmail (e.g., "If you change our room location, we'll quit coming"). Variety may be the spice of life, but people are also creatures of habit. They resist things that cause them discomfort.

Resistance to change is not unique to the church, but the nature of ministry makes managing change especially difficult in the local congregation.

First, we have an unchanging message, and implementing change may appear like we are tinkering with the message. Second, we work with volunteers, and therefore do not have the clout that government, business, or other institutions may have to implement change. Third, the church is a family, and we try not to offend anyone, especially the proverbial weaker brother.

Nevertheless resistance to change will paralyze a congregation if permitted. A church committed to evangelism and edification must use all means possible to point people to Christ and present them mature in Him. While biblical purposes re-

145

main unmovable, the means of accomplishing these purposes must remain flexible. To state it in familiar terms, our commitment is to "function" rather than "form."

While people's resistance should not inhibit church leaders from moving ahead with changes they feel are important, there are several practices that can encourage receptivity to change. Pastors can help their congregations by: creating an atmosphere where change is acceptable; building trust in leadership; making sure a specific change is the best alternative; communicating change early and thoroughly; implementing change carefully, and keeping all lines of communication open during implementation.

Create an Atmosphere Where Change Is Acceptable

Change occurs more easily in a church with a positive and open atmosphere. A healthy atmosphere is one that keeps ministry, rather than methods, before people. It focuses on function, not form. It stresses the positive, not the negative. It holds up the unity of the body of Christ over individualism.

This does not mean that the individual is unimportant, that a time to express something negative is inappropriate, or that all methods are equally good. Rather it is an intentional working together for a united purpose. Brothers and sisters are collaborating to present all people mature in Christ.

Focusing on ministry goals lifts people beyond particulars to see the overarching reason for ministry. An elder may get caught up in his own responsibility, while the club worker only sees Wednesday night. Sermons and Bible studies that review commitment to the Great Commission (Matt. 28), the importance of education, fellowship, worship, and evangelism (Acts 2:42-47), or the necessity of leading people into maturity in Christ (Col. 1:28-29), reminds congregants of the church's unique mission.

Specialized ministries target subpopulations of a congregation. But whether it's the traditional Sunday School, or the crisis pregnancy service, *representing programs as vehicles of ministry* encourages flexibility. Church activities as ends in themselves lose meaning. Singers are not choir members, but leaders of worship; teachers are not managers of instruction, but communicators of truth. Dynamic churches frequently ask: "Are these programs *the best* vehicles for accomplishing ministries goals?"

Fostering healthy discontent also creates an atmosphere where change is acceptable. Advertising companies recognize that people will not move to a different product unless there is some displeasure with their current product. The same is true for the church. For example, Pastor Jahns worked several months with the Christian Education Committee to see the limitations in their Sunday School structure. When they finally presented an alternative format, the church's leadership was already one step closer to adopting it.

Painting a vision of possibilities also keeps the soil of change fertile. "Years from now we may find it necessary to worship on a Saturday evening," Dr. Smith announced to his congregation. The morning theme was worship, and his comment was made to illustrate that worship is not restricted by location or time. But by using this illustration, and many others like it, Roy Smith was subtly opening his people to varieties of ministry possibilities. Some of these ideas, after much lead time, he hopes to implement.

Focusing on ministry goals, representing programs as vehicles of ministry, fostering healthy discontent, and painting a vision of possibilities creates an atmosphere where change is acceptable.

Build Trust in Leadership

People are more willing to follow a leader with integrity. Therefore, establishing credibility in those guiding the congregation is imperative. When a pastor or program leader makes changes too early in a new ministry, he has not given the congregation sufficient time to trust in him. The people don't know if he's really "for them," or if he just wants to do his own thing.

For example, in one town a pastor promised: "Build a church that will seat a thousand, and I'll pack it out every

Sunday." Shortly after the facility was completed, the pastor left. Except for an occasional interdenominational rally, the building is never filled. Each Sunday that congregation enters a visible reminder that pastors can't be trusted. A congregation "burned" by a pastor, is slow to welcome the ideas of a new minister.

The admonition against placing a "novice" in office underscores the importance of credibility. Pastors are better off in early years building trust levels than fighting for innovations. Demonstrating credibility now fosters receptivity later. The magnitude of any change is related to the magnitude of the leadership's credibility. The more unsettling a change (like renaming the church, or modifying its constitution), the higher the leader's credibility for acceptance must be. The pastor's affirmation of leaders and recognition of their faithfulness also makes a congregation more willing to follow their suggestions.

Credibility is also related to the visibility of leadership. *Assuring availability* builds people's trust. When Pastor Gardner arrived at Westside Church he preached from Ephesians on the believer's wealth in Christ. After a year of study, parishioners were heard talking about their position in Christ, and many understood the pastor's task as equipping the saints for the work of service.

While Pastor Gardner's preaching contributed to a healthy church environment, his personal involvement with people was even more motivational. It was in these less formal settings that he learned the needs of his people. Members began to feel that the pastor was "for them." In a similar way he encouraged deacon involvement with their "little flocks." Their personal contacts, and especially acts of kindness during illnesses and times of bereavement drew them closer to the congregation.

Communicating motives helps the congregation understand why specific changes are forthcoming. In less formal settings a pastor is able to share his vision for a dynamic, relevant ministry. In committee meetings, home settings, and during luncheons, he can affirm the church's unchanging purpose, while encouraging innovative methods.

Word of Life Church, located in the Sunbelt, had an ongoing problem with winter attendance increases. The church already had identical worship services at 9:45 A.M. and 11:00 A.M. In the winter months, when many retired folk vacationed in the south, the church would add an 8:15 worship service to its schedule. Unfortunately, the 8:15 service drew very few people, and consequently the attendance bulge at the 9:45 service was not relieved.

To deal with its local situation, the church council decided to schedule the normal church programing at 8:45 and 10:00, adding an 11:15 service in the winter. The rationale was that more people would likely come at the 11:15 time than would come at an earlier 8:15 service. After a six-month trial the unsuccessful new arrangement was dropped, and the old schedule reinstated. Interestingly, throughout that period of change, the church did not seem to suffer in either spirit or attendance.

Why could Word of Life survive that major worship change, while other churches cannot even change their bulletin covers? Several people said it was because they trusted Pastor Dennis, and believed that the staff was trying its best to solve the church's growth problem. Some churches would have mutiny in the pews if the council changed the morning worship service to 10:00 A.M. This church moved into an experiment, and then moved out, without repercussion, because of high trust in its leadership.

Establishing credibility, assuring availability, and communicating motives builds trust in leadership.

Make Sure a Specific Change Is the Best Alternative

The psychologist John B. Watson wrote of the reality of "one-trial learning." For example, if you enter a classroom and sit on the left, the next time you enter the room, you are more likely to sit in that same general location. Over time, these responses deepen and become embedded. Whether or not a given church practice is the best form for accomplishing a biblical function is irrelevant to the person biased by habit. To him the form has meaning because of its association with his worship of God. Therefore, before changes are implemented, leadership must have good assurance that a new suggestion is the best alternative.

Involving those affected by anticipated changes is more than common courtesy. It allows those who feel ownership early input in the process. At times they could shed light on the history that led up to the present structures. Some may also have insights pertinent to a good decision.

But not everybody affected by a change should be part of the implementation process. *Working through a small change team* is more effective. Key leaders related to an issue are best able to strategize, communicate, and implement a change. Coordination and promotion is best accomplished through a representative, yet select smaller group.

Utilizing problem-solving techniques minimizes poor changes. Let me illustrate. Midland Bible Fellowship had a multiple-board system. While the seven boards provided a good check and balance, it was sometimes difficult for the deacon board to give leadership to the church. For example, on one occasion the deacon board recommended expanding the church staff. They hoped that a new associate pastor would not only assist the senior minister, but give special attention to the youth program. The board unanimously approved a recommendation for the expansion, but the trustee board refused to recommend the needed funds to support the position. The trustees' conviction was that the church could not raise the new amount of money.

After a lot of blood, sweat, and tears, Midland Fellowship appointed a constitution revision committee and eventually moved to a one-board system. Its desire was to have one official board (a deacon board) giving oversight to several appointed subcommittees. The only elected officials in the new constitution were the deacons themselves. Now, five years later, the leadership wishes they had more elected officials, and more representation in decision-making. They have seen the organizational structure of other churches in their denomination that use a church council, comprised of ministry (committee) heads. In their haste to move away from a multiple-board system, they chose a one-board system that had little congregational representation. Now, although they would prefer a broader, yet still unified structure, they are afraid to make another change.

Involving those affected by anticipated changes, working through a small change group, and utilizing problem-solving techniques, will assure a specific change is the best alternative.

Communicate Change Early and Thoroughly

One Fortune 500 company has as its employee relations motto, "No surprises." *Conveying ideas in familiar terms* is an essential part of the change process. While many people are offended by a surprise change, they are equally upset by misinformation. Whether a formal presentation in the church newsletter, or a simple verbal description, clarity is essential.

Communicating personally the rationale and implementation strategy for a change goes a long way. A congregational letter may accurately describe a constitution revision, but a personal phone call to clarify questions tells members that the leadership is interested in them personally. In fact, many personal contacts *prior* to a business meeting, will alleviate much of the "venting" that takes place when people feel they have no other platform for voicing their concerns.

Sometimes leaders are in a hurry to make a change and cannot understand why members are dragging their heels. In an attempt to show the value of an innovation, the present situation is sometimes devalued. While fostering healthy discontent does help open people to change, *accepting the feelings of present owners* is a realistic counterbalance. People's feelings are real to them, and leadership must recognize their legitimacy. Giving thanks for what the current form has accomplished in the past, and painting a vision of what the new form could do in the future, wins more allegiance than putting down the former vehicle.

The communication process is also enhanced by *associating innovations with traditional values*. When Valley Community

Church wanted to change versions of its pew Bibles, leaders promoted the importance of using a translation that present members as well as visitors could best understand. "We want people seeking Christ to be able to follow along as the Word is taught," said Pastor Donaldson. While some folks were still unhappy with the change, the transition was relatively smooth because it was linked to the value of more clearly understanding the Bible.

Some leaders err by trying to squelch opposition, but *allowing for disagreement* is a more profitable strategy for long-term acceptance. While a person's *view* is challenged by proposed change, he senses his *worth* is devalued when not allowed to voice his displeasure.

By conveying ideas in familiar terms, communicating personally, accepting feelings of the present owners, associating innovations with traditional values and allowing for disagreement, leadership maintains integrity and the change gains validity.

Implement Change Carefully
The old expression is true: "People can adjust to almost anything if it stands still long enough." The problem arises when we make many changes in a short amount of time.

The more I study congregational life the more I view change as a process that requires time. People are not upset by a new pastor who makes some changes even during the "honeymoon." But they do not want change to overwhelm them. The final step in implementing change may move swiftly, but the overall process—planning, ownership, communication, and implementation—needs adequate time.

Recognizing that people are different is basic to implementation of change. In every congregation there are "innovators," those creative leaders way ahead of the pack. At the opposite end there are those "resisters" who want everything status quo. But the majority of the people fall on a continuum somewhere in between. Some are "early adopters" while others are "laggards," but as a whole this larger middle group will eventually move with the change.[1]

While allowing resisters to express their feelings, large investments of personal time with them is rarely productive. *Winning the support of "legitimatizers,"* however, is critical. These are the people a congregation follows. Whether they are part of the formal structure or informal structure, congregants ask what they think of the change.

For example, one church analyst believes a congregational vote for a pastoral candidate is more related to the integrity of the search committee than with the performance of the visiting candidate. Convincing a congregation that a change is legitimate is more easily accomplished when respected, key people support the move.

Some changes are relatively minor and require little effort to implement. Others need careful study and refinement. *Adopting a trial form first* is one way of maintaining leader integrity, while allowing a congregation to see the merits of the suggestion. For example, one church experimenting with double services decided to implement the change in the spring. The March 1 start-up coincided with the peak attendance period, but also allowed them a three-month trial, since the church would be back to one service during the summer. Knowing that things would be "back to normal" by June helped some people to accept the trial period. The new double arrangement was so successful however, that plans were made to begin the new format on a permanent basis the following September.

In the above example, Williamstown Church respected another important implementation principle. *Evaluating the innovation* was assured because of the trial period. On the first Sunday in May the congregation was surveyed as to the new arrangement. With responses from individuals and feedback from the Christian Education and Worship Committees, the elders were able to make an objective assessment leading to their final recommendation.

People *can* adjust to almost anything that comes their way, if it stands still long enough. By recognizing that people are different, winning the support of "legitimatizers," adopting a trial form first, and evaluating the innovation, careful change assures good change.

Keep All Lines of Communication
Open during Implementation

Good communication helped Heritage Church change one of its long traditions. For more than twenty years its evening service had been at 7:00 P.M. At one of the board meetings Pastor Stubbs asked the deacons to give consideration to the pros and cons of moving the evening service an hour earlier. The initial reason for his suggestion was that a 6:00 P.M. service would benefit the weekly youth fellowship that met after the evening service. The earlier hour would allow the teens to meet in homes and still conclude by 9:30 P.M.

As the board discussed the possible change, they also saw its value for seniors who preferred not to drive after dark, and for families who wanted their school age children in bed early. Though they anticipated some resistance, the board decided to change the hour. The board's decision was made in the winter, but implementation was scheduled for spring, the first Sunday of Daylight Savings Time.

The good lead time between decision and implementation allowed successive issues of the church newsletter to present the rationale for a 6:00 P.M. service. As opportunities arose to talk about the change, the board promoted it enthusiastically. When people expressed their disagreement, the deacons remained cordial, yet reaffirmed the benefits of the earlier hour. The motive for change (a better time for younger families, teens, and seniors) was always kept before the people.

During that first month of change, several families were vocal in their preference for the later hour. For some, it meant the change of dinner scheduling. Others preferred a longer afternoon. As questions came up, the leaders would deal with the issues, avoiding any put-down of the critic. Showing understanding, yet gently pointing to the value of the new hour, they encouraged acceptance. Within a year, people seemed to forget they had ever had a 7:00 P.M. service.

This illustration reveals three principles that Heritage Church handled well. *Anticipating resistance* helped them formalize their rationale and provide enough lead time for acceptance to grow.

Depersonalizing dissent focused disagreement on the issues, not the people. Providing an open ear to those with criticism kept the lines of communication open for clarification and further promotion of the idea.

Affirming the value of the innovation elevated the discussions above traditions and personal preferences to what was best for the families, teens, and seniors in the congregation. Their decision to change, their careful implementation, and their open communication made possible a smooth transition.

Conclusion

Almost everyone believes that change is important. We would rather drive our cars to work than walk; we would rather watch the news on television than wait for a messenger to herald word by foot; and we would rather use our indoor plumbing than the outhouse. Change is not wrong, rather it is helpful.

Too much change, coming too fast, is dangerous. But a blind conservatism is equally detrimental. The Lord's ministers are entrusted with the unchanging Gospel of reconciliation. Their goal is to present all people mature in Christ, and this prioritizes the tasks of evangelism and edification. While these purposes are timeless, changes within our culture continually make possible new ways of accomplishing these goals with greater relevance.

"Is this change really necessary?" That's the question people will ask when a new idea is presented. If a congregation is confident in its leadership, and understands the reasons behind a change, it will likely offer less resistance to a new form that will help the church carry out its biblical functions.

---

[1] These terms are used by Merton Strommen of the Search Institute, but are similar to other writings in the field.

A Checklist for Change

Do our leaders . . .

☐ Create an Atmosphere Where Change Is Acceptable

☐ Build Trust in Church Leadership

☐ Make Sure a Specific Change Is the Best Alternative

☐ Communicate Change Early and Thoroughly

☐ Implement Change Carefully

☐ Keep All Lines of Communication Open during Implementation

CHAPTER TEN

DEVELOPING A HOME BIBLE STUDY MINISTRY

Well, how did it go last week?" asked Ted Ward. Lisa was the first to report: "I have some great news. You know how we prayed that my job situation would be resolved? Well, I talked with my boss, and he's transferring me to the layout department." "Hey! That's great," said John, "I've had good news too! Do you remember how we've been praying for this big project I've been working on? Well, I finished it two days before its deadline, and my supervisor was really pleased."

"I wish I could report some good news," said Randy, "but my job's still a hassle. After the fire last week, I'm sure they want to ax someone in our department for negligence. Besides all this trauma at work, my mom's still in intensive care at St. Luke's Hospital."

Sarah was next to speak: "I wish you'd continue to pray for my new schedule. I've worked it out with the school for the bus to pick up the kids at my mother's house. That way I can drop them off on my way to work and pick them up on my way home. But by the time we get home, finish dinner, and do homework, I'm ready to pass out!"

"Thanks for sharing that, Sarah. Rearing three kids by yourself is a real burden, and we're proud of the way you've been handling it." Ted then asked: "How are things with your mom, Kathy?" "She's finishing up her second round of chemotherapy now, but I still haven't talked to her about Christ. It's funny, I can talk with one of my neighbors about the Lord, but have difficulty in opening a dialogue with my own mom."

Who are these people? Ted Ward's a carpenter who lives with a serious problem. Though only thirty-five years old, he has rheumatoid arthritis, and at times he has trouble holding on to his tools. He wonders what the future holds. Lisa works in a graphic arts department, and her boss had assigned her to a couple of projects with which, as a Christian, she felt uncomfortable. John is a computer programmer who works for one of the large companies in town. Randy works for a large chemical company, supervising one of their major operations. Sarah, recently divorced, just moved back into the work world as a secretary in a downtown office.

These individuals are typical, everyday, ordinary people. But they have something in common. They are Christians who meet together weekly for Bible study and mutual encouragement. Their types of burdens are not exceptional; rather, they are typical of the average person attending our churches. Yet week after week many Christians carry their burdens without anyone else being aware of their hurts.

Why Home Bible Studies

While services of worship and instruction centrally located at the church are important, decentralized small-group meetings in homes are equally profitable for spiritual growth. Small groups provide a *vehicle for Bible study*. While it is possible for people to sit passively during a sermon or Sunday School class, the smaller size of the home Bible study stimulates involvement. A student's preparation for the study, and participation during the study, contributes to better learning.

Home Bible studies typically develop into *cell groups for prayer*. While every member of the church, and every missionary on the field, needs prayer, we usually pray more consistently for people we know personally. The sharing of requests and continued prayer for one another make the group meeting deeply meaningful.

Home fellowships can also become a *means for congregational caring*. Some people make friends easily, but others in the church find it difficult to build relationships. I am not surprised when I hear a person admit, "I've been attending the church for a year now, and I still don't have any friends here." Since this is common for many newcomers, it is essential that we do not leave the bridging of friendships to chance. The congregation that encourages participation in small groups is further along in developing a caring base for its entire membership.

Home Bible studies provide a *format for disciple-building*. We rarely know the maturity level of a person who only attends a worship service. But many Christians who have participated in home Bible studies are able to take those same materials and share them with another person. The process of teaching faithful people, who in turn will teach others, will more likely occur through the small-group format.

The decentralized groups establish *extension sites for ministry*. Many non-Christians will never be drawn into the aquarium called the church. Becoming fishers of men necessitates going out to the waters of our jobs and neighborhoods where non-Christians live. People are won to Christ through participation in a non-threatening, informative Bible study. The homes of our members, and even of nonbelievers, are great ministry sites away from the larger church campus.

Small-group ministries in homes also encourage a *non-professional approach to ministry*. Christians can attend church and listen to a Sunday School teacher, musicians, and pastor without much personal involvement. Corporate services typically require study, preparation, and participation only on the part of the professionals. A church that has a comprehensive home Bible study ministry, however, involves many people in lesson preparation and group participation. Through this structure people begin to understand that they are responsible for their own spiritual development and for growth of one another.

How does a church that is interested in starting a cell group ministry move their plans from the drawing board into homes? The ingredients for a healthy home Bible study program include: a structured program, an assigned study group, an intentional curriculum, a flexible approach, a consistent format, and a trained leadership.

A Structured Program

At First Church the pastor was afraid of home Bible studies. After all, "Who knows what kind of heresy my people may get into?" At best, he thought the groups might end up just a weekly pooling of ignorance: "There is no way to control those groups once they get started; they just turn into cliques disruptive to the church."

Pastor Smith's concern is typical of many ministers, but the benefits of a cell group ministry far outweigh potential disadvantages. In fact, if the program is well-structured it will minimize and even eliminate potential problems. Unfortunately, many programs are started without much advanced planning. Consequently the home cell ministry becomes stagnant, or ceases all together.

A better approach is to first ask questions that will give direction to program planning:

- How long will groups remain together (nine months, two years)?
- How frequently will they meet (weekly, semi-monthly)?
- Who will lead them?
- What will the participants study?
- How can we supervise the groups, and assess people's progress?

At Keystone Church the pastor wanted to begin a home Bible study program, so he first shared his vision and rationale with the board of elders. Upon their approval, Pastor Jim put an attractive description in the church bulletin, inviting people to indicate their interest in joining such a group. As people contacted the church, he personally went to their homes and explained the nature of the program. Pastor Jim told them that the group would meet weekly for nine months (during the school year). He showed them the materials that they would be studying and explained that their participation would require a commitment to weekly preparation.

The pastor was concerned that the first group be a winner. Jim was warned by another pastor of the danger of starting too quickly, or beginning several studies simultaneously. He decided to lead the initial group himself, and through the course of the first year, work closely with someone he was praying would lead another group next year. His plan was to have two groups the following year, and four the year after that. If strong leadership did not materialize, however, he would not sacrifice a quality small group experience, by running several studies poorly.

Since Jim was in touch weekly with his Bible study group, he was able to keep track of how they were progressing spiritually. But as successive groups were begun, he was concerned with supervision of the studies and tracking the spiritual growth of the participants. It was in November that Jim came across an advertisement promoting a conference on small-group ministries. He attended the national seminar and recognized the need for a coordinator for Keystone's growing cell ministry. Jim began to meet monthly with the group leaders, but eventually he turned this position over to John Balanca, his best Bible study leader.

Today Keystone has seven home study groups, and John meets twice a month with the Bible study leaders. At each meeting the leaders give him a written report that updates him on each group. Their report logs the attendance of group members and notes any significant happenings of which the coordinator or pastor should be aware. The strong home Bible study ministry at Keystone Church did not happen by accident. Pastor Jim, the board, and the group leaders answered the five important questions listed earlier. Their ongoing planning and supervision will also assure an effective cell group ministry for years to come.

An Assigned Study Group

Some churches prefer to organize their cell ministry with homogeneous groups, while others prefer groups comprising couples and singles, those newer and older in Christ, and at various stages in life. For example, a church that uses electives in its adult Sunday School may want peers to meet during the weeknight study groups. On the other hand, churches that have a stage-graded adult class, may prefer a cross-stage approach to the Bible study ministry. I have worked with both types of groups and prefer groups with diversity.

When Pastor Lee Smith publicized the start of a new growth group in his church newsletter, twenty people responded with interest. Systematically, he met with them to present the requirements for participation. He then informed them that, if they were willing to make the commitment, he would call them when a new group was formed.

Since Pastor Lee had a couple from his previous group, the Rogers, who were willing to lead a home study, he planned to start two new groups. He wanted to mix the groups because people in different situations can more greatly enrich one another.

Lee made sure both he and the Rogers had singles and couples, those younger and older in age, as well as people newer and older in Christ. For example, Earl and Suzannne Rogers' group included a couple in their twenties, three couples in their thirties, one couple in their fifties, and three singles—two in their twenties, one in her thirties. One of the singles was a woman with two elementary age children; one of the couples in their thirties had just recently come to the church; while the couple in their fifties were charter members.

The diversity in Earl and Suzanne's group was rewarding. Over the course of their two years together they became more than just a study group. They developed into an extended family. An occasional picnic brought their families together, and the group was able to edify and encourage each other in many ways.

An Intentional Curriculum

A structured cell group ministry will give careful attention to the materials used for study. Groups are not formed first, and then asked what they would like to study. Rather, the carefully supervised home ministry will first determine the topics that groups will study. Close supervision of a Bible study program is assured by teacher selection, length of group commitment (a maximum of two years), and by a predetermined curriculum.

While a church may want to establish "fellowship groups," which are loosely structured, "study groups" will have greater intentionality. Home Bible studies should have a purpose for meeting and the purpose reflected in the curriculum. For example, congregants attending a home Bible study for the first time would profit from a Bible basics study. The Navigators *Design for Discipleship* provides seven books which are excellent for a first-year home Bible study. (The contents of this series are delineated at the end of this chapter.) Other quality series include the Fisherman Bible Study Guides, NavPress Life Change Series, Neighborhood Bible Study materials, Churches Alive! materials, and Serendipity studies.

Channeling every first-time participant through a Bible basics course serves two purposes. First, it records who in the congregation has at least one overview of basics essential to the Christian life. Second, it reveals the people capable of leading others through the basics. In fact, a number of people have used Book One of *Design for Discipleship,* in a one-on-one Bible study to lead a nonbeliever to Christ.

After the initial basics Bible study, topics for subsequent studies vary greatly. Groups have studied the Life of Jesus, the Book of Acts, Philippians, or James. There are materials on marriage, money management, evangelism, and personal spiritual development. Course offerings are determined by the expressed needs of people and the collective goals of the church. In the promotion of these subsequent studies, people are reminded that the new groups are only open to those who have completed the basic Bible study.

Materials for group participants are best purchased by the church and distributed through the Bible study leaders. The church that asks individuals to go to a bookstore to purchase the lesson materials can count on some people showing up for meetings unprepared. A better procedure is to maintain a supply of frequently used materials at the church. While this takes an initial outlay of cash, all the expenses of these materials are recovered when class members reimburse the study leader. In addition, people who want to take a friend through a one-on-one study can contact the church when books are centrally located. A structured curriculum helps establish a stable home Bible study program.

A Flexible Approach

People differ from one another, as do their schedules. When I first began to coordinate home Bible studies, my format was fairly rigid. (For example, marrieds were only allowed to join a study if they came as a couple.) But time revealed the advisibility of greater flexibility. Exceptions are beneficial at times. This lesson was impressed upon me during one weekend meeting.

While speaking at a men's retreat, I was surprised to learn that nearly half the group had been Christians less than two years. During our meals together several of the men shared how they had come to know Christ. Most of them had received Christ through men's small group Bible studies.

Up until this time I had always encouraged couples to participate together in studies. My concern was for family time. But this church had discovered that men are less open to talk about Christ (or pray out loud) when they are in a mixed group. While the church had groups for couples, they also provided groups just for men and just for women. Subsequently, I have seen the value of launching men's groups, women's groups, and many mixed groups.

Flexibility is also related to frequency of meetings. While many groups meet weekly, other groups have profited from semi-monthly meetings. Continuity is best in a weekly meeting, but some people simply cannot make that time commitment.

Some pastors who begin home Bible studies hope to eventually substitute them for the midweek service. However, a more flexible approach recognizes that for some people the traditional midweek hour is meaningful, whereas the home setting is uncomfortable. Since home Bible studies are open only to those who make the nine-month commitment, the midweek service also serves for those who can come only irregularly.

To avoid competitiveness, the midweek service can be viewed as one of several study groups. Perhaps there are four groups meeting in homes, an early morning men's group, a Thursday morning women's group, and a Wednesday evening group at the church.

Group leaders, curriculum, and meeting parameters are best predetermined. But since personalities and schedules vary, flexibility in approach encourages both greater participation and more intimate sharing.

A Consistent Format

Once a church has structured its program, composed a new group, and selected its curriculum, it is ready to begin actual weekly meetings. Many working with home Bible studies have found that a two-year *duration of commitment* is beneficial. It can take three to six months for group camaraderie to develop, but group stagnation can occur beyond two years.

Two nine-month terms, with the summer off in between, is an optimal commitment. Many people are reluctant to commit every Thursday evening for two years to home Bible study. People's circumstances change so often that for some a lengthy commitment will discourage them from any involvement. I have noticed that people who have been asked to make a nine-month commitment, and who have found their experience meaningful, will likely make a second nine-month commitment to the same group.

While continuity is encouraged by meeting weekly, some groups have been successful meeting only twice a month. For example, one group that met every other Friday continued together for three years. A group that only meets twice a month will need a longer period (two or three years) to accomplish the goals of the Bible study program.

The *meeting time* of the Bible study should remain consistent. If a 7:30 to 9:30 meeting is best for the participants, then the study should begin promptly at 7:30 for the long-term welfare of the group. A group that delays in getting started will typically delay in closing. When busy schedules press upon group members, and they fear they will not finish until 10:00 or 11:00 P.M., they are more likely to stay home. When the ending hour is honored regularly, members are not afraid to participate, even when their schedules are tight.

A consistent *meeting location* is also beneficial to a study group. Typically, a home is selected for its room size and central location. Some leaders prefer to have a study in their own homes. Sometimes, other factors will determine the location—such as using the home of a couple who has their young children already in bed. Once the site is determined, however, consistency of location will encourage consistency in attendance. If a rotation of homes is involved, a monthly schedule is preferable to a weekly rotation. However, neither encourages regular attendance as much as a permanent location.

A consistent *meeting schedule* will guarantee enough time for study, prayer, and fellowship. Many groups have found it beneficial to begin the evening with Bible study while everyone is fresh. The sharing of praise items and concerns for prayer then leads naturally into intercession. Short, conversational prayer encourages even the timid to participate. Some groups have experienced the benefit of outreach projects, and have worked these into their weekly meetings. Sessions are usually concluded with refreshments. A typical home Bible study schedule would therefore include:

- Bible Study (60 minutes)
- Sharing and Prayer (30 minutes)
- Strategies for Outreach (10 minutes)
- Refreshments (20 minutes)

Consistency in *outreach projects* is energizing to a study group. A group that focuses only on its own needs becomes very introspective and turns stagnant. On the other hand, a group that's always looking for ways to minister to others remains fresh and vibrant.

For example, one group used as its outreach project the sharing of Christ with nonbelievers. The group's goal was to memorize one of the "Four Spiritual Laws" (and supporting references) each month, ultimately sharing the overview with a friend. In another study group, members were challenged to write a note of appreciation to a non-Christian. This not only helped the members express thanks for a specific act of kindness, but helped them build bridges for further sharing. Another home Bible study rented a film on the life of Chuck Colson and then invited friends to a barbeque and showing of the film. Another home group purchased support bars and installed them in the bathroom of a recently handicapped shut-in. Hundreds of such outreach projects will stretch people and infuse enthusiasm into their groups.

A consistent format of Bible study, sharing, prayer, and outreach contributes to an effective home Bible study ministry.

A Trained Leadership

The success of any home Bible study is critically related to the effectiveness of its group leader. The most carefully selected group, using the best materials, in an ideal location, will nevertheless die in the hands of a poor leader. Let me illustrate by introducing you to Jim Wilson and Bill Robinson.

Jim Wilson enjoys the Bible; he has studied it for years. In fact, if you were to ask Jim privately, he would admit that he wishes that he could have been a preacher. When Jim was asked to lead a group, he jumped at the opportunity.

Jim's group started out with great enthusiasm, but eventually members trickled away until only five remained. Jim has a high view of Scripture, and he does not believe doctrinal error is tolerable. Several times he quickly "corrected" answers from his group that did not agree with his view. Jim's comments such as, "No, that's not right; look at the verse again," led some younger Christians to believe they couldn't interpret the Bible.

A leader needs sensitivity and skill to field a wrong answer and move the group to discover the correct answer. Praise for good interpretation builds a learner; rebuke for a poor interpretation discourages him. Unfortunately, Jim felt he had to teach on every issue. He was not really a catalyst or leader; he was a lecturer. It is important for leaders to allow group members to make their own discoveries from the Scriptures, and then praise them for those discoveries. The Bible study exists for the group, not the leader.

By way of contrast, Bill Robinson was concerned that religion not be "forced down people's throats." When he became a home Bible study leader he would often allow his group to wander from the subject of study. Since Bill did not want to offend people, he also overlooked incorrect responses. While the group members enjoyed their time together, they were not leaning how to interpret the Bible. Though Bill's demeanor was opposite that of Jim, he too was an ineffectve teacher.

Leaders must lead; they must take control of their classes. Strong leaders keep their groups on target, yet help them avoid overdependence. Through carefully worded questions, a leader can guide students into discovery and then affirm them for those discoveries.

People recruited to lead home Bible studies should have already participated in groups themselves and have demonstrated leadership capabilities. The Church of the Open Door learned this lesson the hard way. Pastor Jim Thomas had just returned from a conference in Northern California and was excited to develop a home Bible study ministry. In his first year he began two groups; in the second year he added three more. But toward the end of that second year, three of the studies were limping along because he used leaders who were not effective. Trained leadership is essential for a meaningful home Bible study program. The following autumn only two groups were started, but with competent leaders who had participated in previous groups.

The best way to disciple a person for leadership is to let them participate in a group for two years under a good leader—this is the faith community model of learning. In addition, further training is available through a regular meeting of the group leaders. In one church, for example, eleven Bible study leaders met at 8:30 each Sunday for twelve weeks to work through a training manual produced by the Institute of Church Imperatives of Modesto, California. In another church, the Bible study leaders met for eight Sunday evenings (prior to the evening service) to study similar training materials from Churches Alive! of San Bernadino, California.

Both of these churches eventually moved to a once-a-month meeting schedule. In addition to ongoing training, the leaders have found that their time together has produced a healthy camaraderie. They encourage each other and pray together for the members of their groups. Trained leaders who are motivated, encouraged, and affirmed will help assure the success of a home Bible study ministry.

Conclusion

In the early church the believers met together in homes to eat, fellowship, learn, and pray. In fact, for 300 years church sites were in the homes of believers. Today, because of numerical growth, diversified programs, and a culture which associates a bona fide institution with a building, Christians meet on centralized campuses. Yet a warmth and attractiveness still surrounds home meetings.

Large congregational gatherings are great for worship and preaching, and Sunday Schools are profitable for instruction. However, intimacy among Christians is limited in these larger assemblies. While some pastors are fearful of home groups, and others are at a loss as to how to develop them, people still need intimacy, and the church still needs a discipleship program. Many churches serious about edification and evangelism have capitalized on small-group ministries.

Home Bible studies are not just another bandwagon. They are not going to disappear overnight like the busing craze of the mid-seventies. While structure and format may vary from church to church, people will continue to associate together in small groups, just as they did in the early church. And when these small groups meet together visibly, in neighborhoods, not cloistered behind institutional walls, perhaps then, too, community people will see the new life and joy of these believers, and be able to say "the Lord added to their number daily those who were being saved" (Acts 2:47).

A Checklist for Home Bible Studies

Does our church have . . .

☐ A Structured Program

☐ An Assigned Study Group

☐ An Intentional Curriculum

☐ A Flexible Approach

☐ A Consistent Format

☐ A Trained Leadership

Summary of Contents in "Design for Discipleship"

You can learn more about the wealth that is available to you in Jesus Christ through this exciting Bible study series. On your own or in a group you can discover what it means to be a Christ-centered disciple, how to develop Christian character, how to have victory over sin, and how to grow toward maturity in your daily walk with God.

BOOK ONE: YOUR LIFE IN CHRIST

God Cares for You
The Person of Jesus Christ
The Work of Christ
The Spirit within You

BOOK TWO: THE SPIRIT-FILLED CHRISTIAN

The Obedient Christian
God's Word in Your Life
Conversing with God
Fellowship with Christians
Witnessing for Christ

BOOK THREE: WALKING WITH CHRIST

Maturing in Christ
The Lordship of Christ
Faith and the Promises of God
Knowing God's Will
Walking as a Servant

BOOK FOUR: THE CHRISTIAN CHARACTER

The Call to Fruitful Living
Genuine Love in Action
Purity of Life

Integrity in Living
Character in Action

BOOK FIVE: FOUNDATIONS FOR FAITH

Who Is God?
The Authority of God's Word
The Holy Spirit
Spiritual Warfare
The Return of Christ

BOOK SIX: GROWING IN DISCIPLESHIP

What Is a Disciple?
The Responsible Steward
Helping Others Find Christ
Follow-up
World Vision

BOOK SEVEN: OUR HOPE IN CHRIST

An introductory chapter analysis study of 1 Thessalonians

From Design For Discipleship. *The Navigators, P.O. Box 1659, Colorado Springs, Colorado 80901.*

Bible Study Leader's Weekly Report

Leader's Name _____ Date _____
Time meeting started ___ : ___ P.M.
Time meeting dismissed ___ : ___ P.M.
Total number present _____
Lesson location: Book ____ Chapter ____
Those without prepared lessons _____
Names of those absent _____

How did you follow up on both of the above? _____

Which verse(s) did your group memorize this week? _____
Name the people having trouble with memory work _____

Approximate time your group spent in:
    Bible Study _____ Sharing _____
    Outreach Planning _____ Prayer _____
Name the people who this past week:
    Shared their testimony _____
    Shared the Gospel _____
    Led someone to Christ _____
In your observation, is the material covered being applied in the members' daily lives? ___ Give examples _____

List special victories shared by the group _____

List any special problems or special needs that the Pastor/ Church Staff should be aware of _____

What are you doing personally to help this person/couple?

Comments _____

Used by permission of the Institute of Church Imperatives, Modesto, California.

EPILOGUE:
AN OPEN DOOR TO A
NEW WORLD

Recently Grace Church celebrated its twenty-fifth anniversary. Back when the church was founded, its city was less than 45,000 in population. Today over 300,000 reside in this growing community. Then it was the 36th Protestant church established, but now over 132 offer a full calendar of activities.

When Grace's elders met to plan the anniversary, they reflected on how different the world is today from when they began in the 1960s. Less than 5 percent of Americans said they had no religious affiliation back when Grace drew up its constitution. Today over 13 percent of those born after 1957 state they have no religious affiliation. Back then abortions were illegal and AIDS was unknown. In fact, one board member even remembered reading of a scandal in the *New York Times* about a coed at Barnard College living with her boyfriend. Sadly, today that story is not newsworthy.

"Do you remember when our board members were all older married men?" said Frank Jackson to one of his tenured colleagues. "I'm glad we have greater diversity today." The board's current composition includes two seniors, an empty nester, two baby boomers, a single, and two women. The board itself reflects two significant developments taking place in the U.S. as a whole: a growing singles population and an expanding role for women.[1]

When their church began, less than 11 percent of women ages 25 to 59 were unmarried. Today over 25 percent of that age category are single. Then over 50 percent of the married women had traditional families (a working husband, homemaker wife, and two or more children). Today less than 7 percent of the married women live in that arrangement. Women have moved out into all realms of the work force. For example, approximately 500 women had graduated from medical school a generation ago, but today over 5,000 receive their medical degrees annually.

One analyst has pointed out that in the 1960s adults sacrificed for children, but today children are required to sacrifice for adults. Discounts given to children on airlines, buses, and motels now go to seniors. Billions of dollars are transferred annually from taxation into the Social Security system. Inflation, deficit spending, and bond programs eat away the standard of living of the next generation.

While the mission statement of Grace Church and its purposes have remained the same, the world around it has changed significantly. America's social environment has a greater cultural diversity, a more volatile economy, a looser morality, and a changing family structure. The new world is one of growing diversity and complexity.

Some of Grace's board members expressed apprehension about the future. What would their ministry look like in the year 2015? Futurists predict the singles population to grow. Adoptive families, single-parent families, and blended families will increase. For the first time whites will not comprise a majority as more than 50 percent of America's population will be made up of minorities. The disparity between rich and poor will continue to grow, and illiteracy will become especially rampant among city youth. Bio-ethical debates about quality of life will cause tension between the young and old, especially because of the explosion of health care costs and general economic uncertainties.

At that point in their discussion, Pastor Sims interrupted to remind them that effective ministry has flourished in all societal contexts. In fact church history has recorded both the strengthening and expanding of the church through times of persecution and difficulty. "While we live in a new world, a world that is increasing in complexity, I believe the Lord has given us an open door for another twenty-five years of great ministry."

He continued by reminding them how Paul told the church at Corinth that "a great door for effective work has opened for me" (1 Cor. 16:9), and the church at Colosse, "pray for us, too, that God may open a door for our message" (Col. 4:3). Likewise the church at Philadelphia was promised: "These are the words of him who is holy and true, who holds the keys of David. What he opens, no one can shut; and what he shuts, no one can open. I know your deeds. See, I have placed before you an open door that no one can shut" (Rev. 3:7-8).

"I believe that God has opened a similar door of opportunity for us," said the pastor, "but that door, I believe, is in the shape of a cross." He went on to remind them of one of Jesus' teachings: "If anyone would come after Me, he must deny himself and take up his cross and follow Me" (Matt. 16:24). Pastor Sims concluded his comments by affirming: "I'm not sure what challenges will face our community in the year 2015, but I believe if each of us is willing to walk through the cross-shaped door of self-denial, the Lord will honor him here at Grace."

Pastor Sims hit the nail on the head. None of us knows what the future will hold, but we do know that effective ministry requires a faithful commitment of time and talent.

The growing diversity and complexity of our new world is radically reducing our most precious commodity—time. Grade schooler and grandma alike are busy. The minimum wage earner and the executive on the corporate ladder are spent by the end of the week.

The number one Christian education problem facing churches today is finding enough staff for programs. Everyone is busy. Volunteering to serve necessitates a setting aside of some personal goals for the purpose of assisting others. Follow-up of pupils by their teachers also takes time, and that too translates into self-denial. Attending training sessions requires a similar commitment. The work involved in successful church libraries, home Bible study ministries, implementation of change, and coordination of programs requires a valuing of the Lord's work even over some personal ambitions. The attitude of John the Baptist, "He must become greater; I must become less" (John 3:30), has serious time implications for every Christian servant.

Some fear for the future of the church. On the contrary, I'm optimistic! While nominal Christianity in the Western world may decline, the true Church will continue to touch lives even in the darkest recesses of our society. I believe that millions of Christians *will* walk through the door of self-denial. Many of these will find their joy in the educational ministry of the church, following the Lord's commission of "teaching them to obey everything commanded" (Matt. 28:20).

---

[1] See Lyle Schaller's works, especially *It's a Different World*. Nashville: Abingdon Press, 1987.

SELECTED RESOURCES FOR FURTHER STUDY

Bolinder, Garth, Tom McKee, and John R. Cionca. *What Every Pastor Needs to Know About Music, Youth and Education* (Carol Stream, Ill.: Christianity Today, Inc./Word Books, 1986). This book from the Leadership Library Series gives practical help in three prominent areas of church ministry. Recognizing that the senior pastor cannot give full time to each of these areas, the writers focus on the essentials possible for pastoral involvement.

Cionca, John R. *The Trouble Shooting Guide to Christian Education* (Denver: Accent Books, 1986). "This practical volume will help pastors and their associates develop leadership for the total program of the church. It is built on a biblical philosophy and strategy of Christian education. The pastor that is having trouble finding teachers or training them will get immediate help in the *Trouble Shooting Guide*."–Dr. Elmer Towns.

Creative Leadership for Teacher Growth (Elgin, Ill.: David C. Cook Publishing Company, 1982). This resource is a media kit containing all the materials needed for an annual teacher training emphasis. There are three kits in the series, each with four parts for training in summer, fall, winter, and spring. The subjects are relevant, and the leader aids (transparencies, duplicating masters, etc.) are excellent.

Evans, Louis H., Jr. *Covenant to Care* (Wheaton, Ill.: Victor Books, 1982). This book is concerned with building close relationships through covenant groups. Evans defines *covenant* as a solemn promise made by one or more persons who do not intend to break that promise. A covenant relationship implies that whatever we have is available to our covenant brothers and sisters. While leaders and teachers cannot make this type of commitment to every student, they will profit from Evans' presentation on the importance of affirmation, availability, prayer, openness, honesty, sensitivity, confidentiality, and accountability.

Foster, Charles R. *The Ministry of the Volunteer Teacher* (Nashville: Abingdon Press, 1986). "Charles R. Foster shows volunteer church teachers new ways to view their calling. He examines the unique responsibilities, gifts, and skills of volunteer teachers as they carry out their ministry in the body of Christ. Using explicit language and religious concepts, yet presenting them in a highly readable, conversational manner, Dr. Foster relates the practical aspects of teaching to its religious aspects. He points out the threefold purpose of a teacher: to 'bind the generations' of Christians together; to build and nurture the community of faith; to create an environment of caring. Worksheet exercises throughout the book help teachers reflect on key issues and develop strategies for more effective and informed teaching."–Abingdon Press.

Going Up: Lifting People to New Heights in Bible Study (San Bernadino, Calif.: Churches Alive!, 1978). This eighty-four-page paperback is designed to train leaders for home Bible studies. "Growth Groups" typically meet one night a week for approximately two hours of in-depth Bible study, prayer, fellowship, and outreach planning. Study of this book will help Bible study leaders motivate their groups, formulate good questions, maintain control, and build enthusiasm.

Hendee, John. *Recruiting, Training, and Developing Volunteer Adult Workers* (Cincinnati: Standard Publishing, 1988). "The prospects of working with adults is terrifying to many people in the church. They'll work with children, or they'll work with teens, but they are literally scared to death of the idea of working with adults. This book will help you solve that problem. Here you will find out how to: determine your purpose and program accordingly; determine what positions you need to fill to minister effectively; recruit and train people to serve in your program; support and develop your workers; and plan effectively for ministry activities and programs."–Standard Publishing

Hendricks, Howard. *Management* (Costa Mesa, Calif.: Vision House, 1974). This six-cassette tape series deals with organizing, motivating, planning, leading, and managing time. These lectures, originally given to Campus Crusade for Christ staff members, are helpful to all in leadership. The content of Hendricks' material is excellent, but the highlight of the series is the motivational lift received from listening to Hendricks. His enthusiasm is contagious.

Hendricks, Howard G., and Charles R. Swindoll. *Survival for the Pastor* (Portland, Ore.: Multnomah Press, 1981). This six-cassette tape album was recorded at the Multnomah Pastors Enrichment Congress. The messages by Swindoll and Hendricks encourage pastors who may be on the brink of burnout, and focus on priorities for a healthy ministry. "Being Yourself," "Danger Signals for Leadership," and "The Effective Minister in This Decade" are just three of these practical addresses.

The Institute in Church Imperatives (Modesto, Calif.: First Baptist Church of Modesto, 1987). Twice a year the First Baptist Church of Modesto hosts an Institute of Church Imperatives and an Institute of Child Education. These comprehensive seminars focus on the total ministry of a local church. They deal with purpose, organization, implementation, staffing, job descriptions, methods, and evaluation tools. A "How To" manual is provided for each registrant, but the process (experience) of the week-long seminar, is of primary value. A pastor interested in seeing a positive model of dynamic ministry would profit by taking church leaders to these seminars.

Johnson, Douglas W. *The Care and Feeding of Volunteers* (Nashville: Abingdon Press, 1978). "Volunteers, whether they be Sunday School teachers or church ushers, are vital to the life of the local church. Recent in-depth studies reveal that 30 to

65 percent of local church members are willing to serve their respective churches in some sort of volunteer capacity. Douglas Johnson explores the unique motivations, ambitions, and needs of these valuable individuals, emphasizing what makes a volunteer want to work, and what gives him/her non-monetary satisfaction. He discusses how to identify, recruit, and train volunteers; how to enable and motivate them; how to assign appropriate tasks; how to help plan their work; and how to enable them to recruit and train other volunteers." –Abingdon Press.

Lead Out: A Guide for Leading Bible Discussion Groups (Colorado Springs, Colo.: NavPress, 1974). *Lead Out* is designed to train new Bible study leaders and to improve the leadership skills of veterans. Though primarily designed to work as a companion to Navigators study materials, its principles are transferable to work with any group. Solid guidance is given on methods, roles that people play in discussion, and turning problems into opportunities. Home Bible study coordinators could profitably use this book for weekly training with group leaders.

Lovorn, Tom and Janie. *Building a Caring Church* (Wheaton, Ill.: Victor Books, 1986). The authors offer a plan for developing a care ministry within a local church. The strategy includes shepherding those who attend the congregation, as well as reaching those in the community. A care coordinator (essential to the program) maintains records, advertises, and trains people for the ongoing ministry of caring.

McDonough, Reginald M. *Working with Volunteer Leaders in the Church* (Nashville: Broadman Press, 1976). "No matter how competent and popular the church staff may be, church growth and ministry ultimately depend on volunteer leaders. Wise is the pastor who recognizes this and uses a good part of his energy in discovering and training them. This book offers practical guidance for the whole spectrum of that ministry; enlistment, motivation, introducing new ideas, establishing goals, and so on. It is based on sound principles of interpersonal relationships and on varied church experience. It can be helpful, therefore, in all churches."–Broadman Press

Marlowe, Monroe, and Bobbie Reed. *Creative Bible Learning for Adults* (Ventura, Calif.: Regal Books, 1977). This International Center for Learning Handbook is one of three books (also texts for children and youth) designed for both new and experienced teachers. It explains stages of adulthood and describes characteristics of adult learning. Its primary emphasis is on learner involvement in the teaching process. The learning cycle (approach, explore, discover, and appropriate) is practically illustrated. The second part of the book deals with organizing the adult class for both learning and shepherding.

Perry, Charles, Jr. *Why Christians Burn Out* (Nashville: Thomas Nelson Publishers, 1982). The people more likely to experience burnout are the dedicated, committed, high-achieving, helpers. Since these personality types also serve in the church, leadership must give careful attention to recognizing burnout symptoms (rather than increasing stressors). The book offers positive hope for those experiencing burnout. It offers suggestions for relieving stress and restoring zeal.

Roadcup, David. *Recruiting, Training, and Developing Volunteer Youth Workers* (Cincinnati: Standard Publishing, 1987). "Inside this book . . . you'll find answers to questions like these: What should I look for in volunteer workers? How do I ask people to volunteer? What do I do if they say no? How do I train them? What's the difference between training and developing youth workers? There's more! Not only does this book give you a clear presentation of what you need to be doing in the areas of recruiting, training, and developing, it also shows you how! There is even curriculum for your training sessions—complete with outlines and transparency masters!"–Standard Publishing

Rush, Myron. *Management: A Biblical Approach* (Wheaton, Ill.:

Victor Books, 1986). Rush defines management as "meeting the needs of people as they work at accomplishing their jobs." The pastor or program leader is not just trying to "use" people to accomplish his program, but rather to serve people by helping them find meaningful areas of ministry. With this approach to ministry in mind, the author then explains the practices of planning, decision-making, problem-solving, communication, delegation, time management, attitude, performance, performance evaluation, and the resolving of conflict. Rush's emphasis on matching the right people with the right assignment is not only key for successful delegation, but is important to avoid worker burnout. His emphasis on evaluating our work through annual reviews is a must for churches.

Schaller, Lyle E. *Activating a Passive Church* (Nashville: Abingdon Press, 1981). Church researcher Lyle Schaller diagnoses the causes of church passivity and formulates methods for combatting the problem. The passive church is characterized by loss of enthusiasm, devisiveness, and a lack of goals. These churches have low self-esteem, poor physical care of their buildings, heavy dependence on the pastor, a strong past-orientation, a lack of adult participation, and frequently, a domineering and intimidating lay leader. However, Schaller believes there is hope for the passive church and lays out a game plan for its revival. Among his suggestions, he stresses the role of the senior pastor in the renewal process.

Schaller, Lyle E. *Assimilating New Members* (Nashville: Abingdon Press, 1978). This is another practical book, with application for any congregation. Schaller deals with many of the do's and don'ts of bringing members into a church fellowship, and then keeping them active. Many churches are unconsciously set up to exclude visitors. For example, strong inclusiveness and cohesiveness may actually make newcomers feel unwelcome. Using a wealth of case studies (typical of Schaller), he moves from analysis of the problem to requisites for assimilating new members.

Schaller, Lyle E. *Looking in the Mirror* (Nashville: Abingdon Press, 1984). As the title would imply, the author's purpose is to help leaders evaluate the ministry of their congregations. In Section 1 (chapters 1–4), Schaller raises general questions about the distinctive nature of the worshiping congregation. Section 2 (chapters 5–11) analyzes the dimensions of congregational life from turning points in the past to the characteristics of present members. In Section 3 (chapters 12–14), he highlights assumptions specifically related to youth ministries, weekday nursery schools, and building planning committees. Any congregation doing a self-study would profit from a look into Schaller's mirror.

Schaller, Lyle E. *The Small Church Is Different!* (Nashville: Abingdon Press, 1982). "God must love the small church—he made so many of them." This is Schaller's conclusion as he shares his enthusiasm for the smaller church. His twenty distinctions between small and large churches are right on target. Small churches are not just smaller versions of larger churches—they are unique. Understanding their differences will help pastors and lay workers in smaller churches maximize their uniqueness.

Senter, Mark, III. *Recruiting Volunteers in the Church* (Wheaton, Ill.: Victor Books, 1990). "How *do* you get the gifted people to volunteer for ministry opportunities in the local church? Let's be honest. The problem of recruiting volunteers is perhaps the most aggravating and least rewarding of all the ministries in the local church. To make matters worse, all too often when the recruitment task is completed workers resign— perhaps for good reasons—and the process starts all over again. So what is a church to do to solve the recruitment hassle? *Recruiting Volunteers in the Church* includes step-by-step procedures and an abundance of resource materials for the recruitment process. Drawing on his years of experience, the author creates situations in which Pastor Jeff is able to exemplify a blend of spiritual gifts and management skills to accomplish his primary assignment in the book—the recruitment of a strong staff of volunteers for Walnut Heights Church."–Victor Books

Shelly, Marshall. *Well Intentioned Dragons—Ministering to Problem People in the Church* (Carol Stream, Ill.: Christianity Today, Inc./Word Books, 1985). This first book in the Leadership Library Series takes a candid look at "dragons," those people who, though often well-meaning and sincere, seem to undermine the ministry of the church. From time to time each leader must work with difficult people, and Shelly helps the reader learn how to minister even while under attack. Though primarily for pastors, this book encourages all leaders in dealing with power struggles. It shows how to keep church disagreements from turning into holy wars. Developing trust, and building a positive atmosphere, decreases dragons. Yet even in their presence, leaders can learn and grow through their criticism.

Smalley, Gary and John Trent. *The Blessing* (Nashville: Thomas Nelson Publishers, 1986). This book deals with the Old Testament concept of "blessing." The blessing includes: meaningful touch, spoken words expressing high value, picturing a special future for the recipient, and commitment. The authors show the devastating effect on the individual who has not received his or her parental blessing, and the rewards of the positive enactment. While their primary audience is parents, there is also application to friends and church members. For example, each teacher can pass on a blessing with students and each program coordinator with the teaching staff.

Stewart, Ed, and Nina Fishwick. *Group Talk: A Complete Plan for Leading Adult Bible Discussion Groups* (Ventura, Calif.: Regal Books, 1986). The authors are concerned with helping adults develop "informal group conversation which is centered on a Bible text and directed toward a meaningful goal." The leader is viewed as a catalyst, guide, clarifier, and affirmer; therefore the discussion method is superior because it: enhances retention of information, encourages value formation, develops questioning skills, creates a sense of community, affirms each participant, taps into learner experiences, and provides needed feedback. Bible study leaders will find practical suggestions for typical group problems such as no response, monopolizing, irrelevant or wrong answers, and disagreements. This paperback is an excellent tool for ongoing training sessions with Bible study leaders.

Stewart, Yvonne. *You Can Find Teachers* (Nashville: Abingdon Press, 1988). "This inexpensive, handy how-to-do-it guide offers you proven-effective ideas, a practical framework, and usable materials for successfully recruiting local teachers. Included in this all-in-one booklet are: a photocopyable text for two bulletin inserts; a letter of commitment for teachers; clip art for newsletters and bulletins; and a logo for your recruitment campaign."–Abingdon Press

Stubblefield, Jerry M., ed./comp. *A Church Ministering To Adults* (Nashville: Broadman Press, 1986). Adults presently make up 73 percent of the U.S. population, so today's churches can ill afford to pursue strategies that only focus on children and youth. Dynamic, growing churches are churches that have vibrant adult ministries. The four parts of this book deal with adult life cycle (chapters 1–7); meeting needs of adults through programs (chapters 8–14); how adults learn (chapters 15–17); and challenge of adult Christian education (chapters 18–21). A church glories in its children, but depends upon adults for leadership, money, wisdom, and know-how. Stubblefield brings into focus the New Testament pattern of Christ, with a high vision for the task of adult education.

Westing, Harold J. *Evaluate and Grow* (Wheaton, Ill.: Victor Books, 1976). Evaluation is something that is done every Sunday by those who visit our churches, yet most pastors and C.E. directors avoid making an honest assessment of their own ministries. Evaluation is not negative or positive—it simply reveals the facts. If there are biblical mandates to follow, and church goals to pursue, then evaluation helps the congregation measure its success. Westing presents seven laws of "quantitative growth," and then offers seven laws of "qualitative growth." His book is full of helpful guides and evaluation forms for self-study.

Wilson, Marlene. *How to Mobilize Church Volunteers* (Minneapolis: Augsburg Publishing House, 1983). The average parish sees only a handful of people serving in ministry, while the rest come to watch on Sunday. The author's theological conviction leads her to conclude that all have been created, called and equipped to be God's people, and therefore are expected to act accordingly. Wilson identifies problems which inherently have restricted who ministers, and then discusses the importance of leadership, motivation, climate, and organizational systems to enhance involvement. Both professional staff and lay leaders will benefit from this book. Chapter four on implementing a volunteers' ministry program is especially helpful.

INDEX

190